KYRIE
Letters to a Friend

KYRIE
Letters to a Friend

Charles Trueheart

Houghton Mifflin Company Boston
1971

FIRST PRINTING   R

International Standard Book Number:
0-395-12108-6
Library of Congress Catalog Card Number: 71–132334
Printed in the United States of America

The lines from "Farewell to Miles" are reprinted
with the permission of Farrar, Straus & Giroux,
Inc., from *Short Poems* by John Berryman, copy-
right 1948 by John Berryman. The poem "Ultimately" by Ernest Hemingway, on page 159, is
reprinted by permission of the Estate of Ernest
Hemingway.

A Gift of Grace for *Ted*

. . . McPherson in the Chinese sun
May achieve the annihilation of his will;
The urbane and bitter Miles at Harvard may
Discover in time an acid holiday
And let the long wound of his birth be still.

Possibilities, dreams in a crowded room.
Fantasy for the academic man,
Release, distinction. Let the man who can,
Does any peace know, now arise and come
Out of the highballs, past the dog, forward.
(I hope you will be happier where you go
Than you or we were here, and learn to know
What satisfactions there are.) No one heard.

John Berryman
from "Farewell to Miles"

Foreword

AT THE BEGINNING of my junior year at the Phillips Exeter Academy, I walked into a classroom to attend the first session of a contemporary ethics seminar. Sitting at the head of the table was a man I had never seen before. He was the new school minister and his name was Edward Stone Gleason.

The course was a fairly good one and taught me something about how people are with each other, something I hadn't really thought about before. But it was distinguished particularly by the teacher. As the New England autumn sank into winter, I drowsed through some classes; in Gleason's I stayed awake. One day he and I discussed a short story by John Updike called "The Music School" and it seemed that we were the only people in the room.

Whatever was sparked that day continued, grew, and intensified. Together, Gleason, seventeen other students, and I became the deacons who conceived of and organized services every Sunday afternoon in what might be called a contemporary idiom. That experience first made me aware of a potential future in a new kind of ministry. Yet there was something more, usually unspoken, between Gleason and me. As the spring of my senior year approached, the opportunity arose to work on an off-campus project. I asked an Episcopal minister in Washington, my hometown, if I could come to work as an intern, and he agreed. Gleason and I talked about ways of recording my "educational experience" and decided the best way was for me to communicate through letters to him what was happening to me while I was away — weekly reports of my views on the contemporary church.

It was obvious to me as soon as I wrote my first letter (before I even started work) that the letters would not be restricted to my project. They would be as close to a conversation with Gleason as they could be, and they would try to include my feelings about anything I felt like writing about. Ideally they would be written almost every day. All of this — and a perception that Gleason was the closest friend I had ever had — happened spontaneously.

When I returned to school in early May to begin working at a small church in the next town, I continued to write. Every morning before breakfast I walked to Gleason's office in the school church and stuffed a few pages under his desk blotter. Sometimes the same afternoon, a typed response would appear in my post office box.

It rained on my last night at school, and my friends and I graduated in the sunshine the next morning. I left Exeter, and I left Gleason, but now I called him Ted. I lived in Paris that summer, and wrote to him still, letters about the time. The summer, I think, pointed me a certain way and gave me a little push.

When I came back to the United States, I went off to

college. Soon after I said good-bye to my family, who were leaving for Africa. The last day I saw them, I wrote my final letter to Ted. It is the last one in this book. I have grown since then; perhaps a better word is that I have moved on. But these feelings, these letters are real and undeniable. They are about a stage, if you want them to be, or a process, if you prefer that image.

I have people to thank. Perhaps the most important are the people I won't name, the ones who make up this book, most of whom didn't know that I would write about them when they were with me. And greater appreciation to the ones who knew and still trusted me. Peter James Lee, who told me that my writing was good, and Shannon Purves at Houghton Mifflin, who led me into the world of publishing with patience and kindness. Bill and Phoebe Trueheart, who made me and then let me be myself, with reassuring smiles. And Ted and Anne Gleason, who cared.

I wrote this foreword sitting in the Bois de Boulogne, a park in Paris where I spent four years of afternoons and Sundays when I was a little boy. Nearby is an amusement park and a little zoo. I remember it all very clearly — running around in my own fantasy world. While I sat and worked, a little French boy ran up to me, brandishing a silver six-shooter and saying, "J'ai six balles dans ce pistolet et elles sont reservées pour vous." He shot me twice. No moral. I just wish it could leave me more gently.

C.T.

Neuilly-sur-Seine, France

Contents

Washington

One

March 22, 1969

EIGHT-YEAR-OLD brother in one hand, the sweat of newness in the other, I walked into dark (contrast from sunny outside) St. John's this morning, to the 11 A.M. service, with John C. Harper preaching. We were led down the plush, carpeted aisle by a distinguished gentleman. When we sat down, the hymn had begun, but I knelt on the cushions and prayed. If that beginning prayer is called anything, which it shouldn't be, for the first time ever, with all the anticipation I could have, it meant something. The thoughts that ran through my head had a unity of looking-forwardness. I had arrived at a new home, and singing, head bowed, in white and gilt robe, was my new Father, very different from the Rev, yet sharing the same informal piety, the same contemporary understanding, the same emotional and intellectual open-mindedness that I perhaps need. I stood and began to sing, and noticed the voices were too high, too feminine, and that my adolescent squawk was not hidden by other adolescent squawks, but was painfully revealed in

its clash wth lilting voices of girls and old ladies. Yes, the old
ladies would be my biggest problem; I saw them everywhere,
not a hippie in sight, only fur and perfume, and veils, and
new me in the middle.

I mumbled my way through the confession and thanks-
giving which everyone knew but me. I knew some of the
phrases, but not all, and I told myself to learn them soon
lest I be excommunicated. Harper's sermon was dramatic,
traditional: an interesting story from his personal life, a slow
dissemination of "you have probably had the same experience" and then ten minutes of intensive morality. The subject
was the value of the old to guide us through the pain of the
new. We find security in falling back to what is past when
we are faced with the insecurity of what is to come. I cannot
dispute it, but there is much left out, and I must take it up
with Harper if I ever get the chance to talk with him. I
thought about Mr. Gleason's words, that maybe I had something to offer as well as being offered something myself. I
also thought about your words about Harper hurting inside.
That made me feel warm and close to him, but I wanted to
find it out myself. The service was neat, almost programmed,
and I had a hard time keeping up with it. Too many people
knew exactly what to do, exactly how to feel, and this challenged me. Suddenly I felt maybe I was ahead of them, that
they were not even conscious of the fact that they could not
keep up with me, and then I could not find my place in the
Book of Common Prayer and I was defeated. "As it was in
the beginning, is now, and ever shall be, world without end.
Amen." I hoped first for the truth of the part about the
world, and then for the flexibility of the preceding parts. I
hoped for an open-mindedness and perhaps a shedding of

exactitude and oblivious comfort of participating in a service. Perhaps a little pain would have been appropriate. A thought came to mind: Charlie, grab the hand of that old lady next to you and bow your head and pray and hope and — pop — no that would never do. We must work within the system to change the system. I am not disillusioned, merely impatient. Keep the faith.

Then it was neatly, precisely over. I walked into the sun, in line with the people shaking Harper's warm, dry hand Hello. The sun glared off the balding part of Harper's head, and he kept smiling. He was pleased to see me; his handshake was close. He took me aside, dropping the precision of courtesy for the uneasiness of friendship, and told me to come right to him tomorrow morning. "We have exciting things in store for you." I beamed, the mustache itched, and I was gone into the parish house for coffee, a cigarette, and a pleasant chat with an acid head acquaintance from Brooks. (He: "God, how did you get roped into this bag? I can't even face this scene straight." CT beamed and said he was working here on his project and CT knew the acquaintance would never be quite as zonked as CT was then on hope itself.) I found Josh, with a picture postcard from Sunday school, with all the books of the Old Testament and New Testament listed in order. ("Look at the sixth one, Charlie." He handed it to me: yes, the Book of Joshua.)

Home to lunch with cousin Warren, wife, grandson, son, and another, unidentified, woman. A trying time: adolescence, middle age, senility all trying to mesh. Neither of the two eldest could get up from our couch without help. No wine for lunch, they are too old. I sat next to Mrs. Unidentified at the table and the conversation finally out of despera-

tion got around to my project. She had just been to church
at St. Mark's, run by a man named Hawkins. The woman was
very impressed ("They played some Joan Baez record") and
we had a good talk about worship. I must find out how
Hawkins does it with lots of old people. I feel like some
theological Cupid trying to match up Pope Paul with Ted
Gleason.

I repeat: it is a time of real hope, of effort, of patience.
I am ready.

March 24, 1969

FIRST DAY of work. Arrived late as instructed, and had a long
talk with Harper. I was impressed with the amount of time
that had been spent preparing for my arrival. Harper was
extremely open with me, and almost began with the words
"I'm not going to apologize for Saint John's, even though it's
vastly different from your church at Exeter. It has a lot to do
with where we are and who we are dealing with. But at the
same time we remain open to your ideas, and I want you to be
perfectly candid with me at all times, as I will be with you."
At which point he told me that I ought to wear a tie around
the parish house. Yes. But I am very happy. I have my own
desk on the third floor next to a new secretary who is anything but gorgeous. The two assistants are open and friendly,
and I will be working directly under Peter Lee, the community minister. When I arrived, he produced a schedule
for the week and a sheet of information. I will be doing
everything under the sun: three weeks of work in the morning at St. Philip's in Anacostia; calling with Mr. Blayney
Colmore, the parish minister; working with a man named

Mr. Raymond on St. John's new fund drive, painfully remi-
niscent of the one at school but at least worthwhile; and
general office work, for which I will learn to operate the
mimeo and Addressograph machines tomorrow; and last but
not least, running errands, the first of which I just returned
from — picking up Harper's car at a nearby garage. My first
experience of the day was about half an hour after I arrived.
Harper got a call from Georgetown University Hospital
about a patient he knew who had open heart surgery last
week. So the two of us ran off to the hospital to see him. We
had good talks on the way over and back about the differ-
ences in city parishes as opposed to school and hospital
parishes. Harper said he thrives on the variety of daily
experience and is glad he got out of the school circuit, which
is where he began.

At lunch I attended a men's luncheon, the purpose of
which was to acquaint male members of the parish with the
work of the church and with the development program
(goal: $750,000). I felt somewhat out of place in a room
with twenty distinguished businessmen and government officials, but I ran into one I knew and one who seemed interested in what I was doing, so all was not lost. But I certainly
looked a lot different from them. I am staying over (I am
now still at work, taking advantage of an empty electric
typewriter) to attend my first vestry meeting at five. From
what I have been told about vestry meetings, I may get
enraged at these illustrious gentlemen this evening. But trust
me, I remain conscious of my context, and am rapidly inte-
grating myself into the nine-to-five.

✿

Five o'clock weariness slowly dribbled into the conference room. Hot pink faces, all looking fairly self-important yet amused, drifted into the tea and cookies area, and then to various dark wooden chairs around the heavy table.

The meeting was concerned almost totally with the development campaign. For the first time I saw that everyone but possibly Mr. Lee and myself was completely enthusiastic. The eyes and nostrils of these good Christians came alive at the first mention of a fund drive and the amount to be reached in two months, hoping (I thought too optimistically) that each parishioner would give $333 as opposed to the statistical $200 per annum of past years, thinking (rather unimaginatively I thought) that various names would suit the campaign better than others — A Three-Year Program for St. John's was the name finally decided upon. I had thought of several: Triple Thrust for '72 and more modestly St. John's in 1972: The Triple Program, but suggested neither. First day jitters die slowly.

The vestry meeting leaves me only with questions. To what extent is the work of these men, the vestry, an act of faith? Is my skepticism at their motivation an indication of my own lack of faith? If these men were and are really engaged in some sort of act of faith, in some financial sacrament, why the aura of a board meeting at General Motors? I was left with two thoughts: either the vestrymen could not escape their everyday mold and saw the drive as another financial adventure, or their life of faith meant a total commitment, an ultimate concern for any object of their involvement. In the meeting I was conscious of these two things as opposites, but now they strike me as much the same thing. As I hope you gathered, the first alternative was meant to be unfavorable, the second favorable; but as I look now, they can both be taken either way, and are thus the same. I hope I am making sense.

March 25, 1969

TODAY, had there been any, I would tell you solely of my thoughts. There were none — today has been beautifully practical and dismally unprofound. I drove around the city this morning, attended the second of the men's luncheons, and this afternoon learned how to use the Addressograph, the Xerox, the postage machine, as well as addressing and stamping envelopes, copying off some music for the choir director, and running off a letter for Mr. Harper. But I have gained widespread recognition here for my ability to do such things so I may be doing quite a bit of this before my time is through. They also found out I could type.

I did have an interesting talk with Mr. Lee this morning (I am beginning to feel that he will be the only one who can help me or understand me) about what I'm going to be doing, and I told him I wanted to be in some services, which is, as I saw rather quickly, quite a demand. But he said he was planning already for the memorial services for Eisenhower and that he would want me to help him with those. So I may be doing something in the church building after all.

I have gotten the impression from the three things that I have written you that I am sounding rather unimpressed, cynical, intolerant, and a host (yuk) of other complaints. Untrue. It's just that what few complaints I do have I am afraid to voice to my bosses, and must therefore vent my wrath on poor you.

In case you see Mr. Herney, you might tell him that it looks as though I will be getting my paper in on time, but that I couldn't find some of the sources that I originally wanted and I have little time to write the damn thing. Funny, I always had plenty of spare time at school. Now that I think about it, don't breathe a word to Herney.

March 26, 1969

THE STERILE HOSPITAL corridors were busy with custodians, nurses, doctors, interns and patients on stretcher-carts. The Reverend C. Blayney Colmore and I were visiting an old lady who had suddenly developed something. When we finally found her room, he went in before me, and I waited in the hall, eying the workers, who paid little attention to me. Colmore came out with his usual good-natured smile and told me that she ought not to be visited, that she had a tube running down through her nose and could barely talk. My stomach turned and I told him I was squeamish and would have to get over that kind of thing. He was kind and assured me that he still hadn't. Colmore is a wonderful man, and is perfect for his job, which is calling on the sick and old. He is sincere, almost painfully so until you get to know him. We left the hospital and proceeded to an address in northwest Washington, about three blocks from my house. Our conversation was about going to see sick people, and how the fact that we didn't speak to the old lady is unimportant. He told me honestly of his feelings toward his work, which are that he loves it.

The house on Indian Lane was dark. We chuckled at the old magazines piled up in the window as we rang the doorbell. A foreign maid came. We identified ourselves, and she disappeared, leaving us on the doorstep. Finally, an aged woman came to the door and stuck her head into the light. "Yes?" We told her who we were and she let us in, dark, unlit hallway, thick tapestries hanging over doorways. I shook her hand: gnarled, maybe with arthritis. We went into a simple, dim living room and she told us to sit down. She was quite deaf, as she had said in her letter, which had arrived at the parish house that morning, containing a check for $100 and a note: "Enclosed is our Easter gift for St. John's. We are too old and too deaf to come to church any longer, but we always loved it when we went, and enjoy reading the bulletin every week." Colmore said, "We are going to see them," and there we were, in her living room. She sat on the couch as Colmore and I shouted idle questions at her. It was all uneasy, but I could tell she was warm and intelligent and still sharp for her age, I would guess late seventies. Her fingers, almost like jelly, quivered as she gestured with her hand.

She: "Oh, yes, we were in the Foreign Service, in Athens, London . . . what more could you ask in wonderful places like that?"

Colmore: "WHEN DID YOUR HUSBAND RETIRE, MRS. ELIOTT?"

She: "Oh, long ago . . . why, he's eighty-two now . . . he's off at a luncheon, I think, but he should be back. After all, he's old."

I was mystified and awe-struck. I was so young, and I thought so intelligent, and she so old and so sharp. Here we were in some sort of Edward Albee play, shouting, and loving each other with each word. And the husband. I cannot describe what kind of man he is. Like an old trickster from *The Wizard of Oz* or something. Eyebrows up and down. An index finger shot out with a grin to make a point. Wonderful eyes sunk deep in a freckled forehead, vibrant, expressive, behind vague wrinkles. I saw him as I looked over my shoulder. He was standing past some curtains in the kitchen doorway. He saw me sitting there, he had no doubt been watching me, and he smiled when I saw him. I stood nervously and said, quavering (I suppose to Colmore but for general information): "I think Mr. Eliott is here . . ." and Colmore rose as he entered the room.

He: "How do you do?"

Me: "I'm Charlie Trueheart, I'm . . ."

Colmore: "HOW DO YOU *DO*, MR. ELIOTT. I'M BLAYNEY COLMORE FROM ST. JOHN'S CHURCH. WE JUST CAME OUT TO THANK YOU FOR YOUR GENEROUS *CHECK* AND TO *CHAT* WITH YOU AWHILE."

He: "So pleased . . . mmm . . . sit down, sit down." He sat on the couch and brushed his wife's hand, smiling at her.

He: "I was just feeding the cats, you can always tell when they're hungry, meow, meow."

She told him that my father was in the Foreign Service and had lived in Vietnam, which I had told her before, and he gave me the same response as she did: What should we do over there? I said I had no opinions, and he said I was a man after his own heart, smiled, lifted his eyebrows, stuck a finger at me, and grinned. Trueheart beamed. We talked, happily, for five minutes about Vietnam, each taking turns expressing our own views. I agreed with everyone since I

had no opinions: yes, exactly. Colmore talked about in-
humanity, and I about the Vietnamese character and both of
them about history, their intellectual diet I suppose. The
room was filled with books and magazines which I could
picture them reading all the time. She spoke of reading
things that came by the "post" and I didn't realize until later
that she meant the mail and not the *Washington Post*. She
was old, and he, eighty-two. She said something about what
her father had told her about war, and she interjected that
he had been too young to have fought in the War. I assumed
that it was the First until she said it was the Civil and I
nearly sank to the floor. No, it was not surprise, but some sort
of sudden awareness of how terribly young I was, and how
little I had to tell, and how much they had to tell but
couldn't because no one could see them and no one would
talk to them. I suddenly wanted to spend a month draining
them of tales of Washington in 1920, Athens in 1930, and all
that I will never be able to live no matter how hard I try. I
almost feel doomed to mediocrity in the world I am in. There
is so little that is physically unexplored. Everything seems
used up. I was born fifty years too late, and I will never be
able to see Washington with countryside about where the
cathedral is now, and trees growing where my living room is
now, and people playing baseball right smack in the middle
of the 1300 block of F Street. I am sad, but happy to have
spent moments with some terrific old people, who are near to
death but fully alive. We finally stood, and Colmore said we
should go and God bless them, and I was almost speechless,
mumbling loudly a good-bye, and stepped from the dark into
modern Spring Valley. I said they were wonderful and he

said yes, the strength of that talk would keep him going for days. Silence and then as we got into the car: "You know, Charlie, so many ministers bitch about calling on old people and I think that's just pure shit."

March 27, 1969

DRIVING DOWN, down, down, speeding down a curving street. At a bend, flush against the trees, thonged to a beagle, black stockings, green skirt lifted slightly in the breeze, black sweater and long golden hair, and I drove by this ravishing creature fast, and craned sideways to see its face. It was she who had peered so long ago over the steering wheel and said good-bye, and she who had been a bitch at the glittering Chevy Chase Club at Christmastime, and she who had played tennis with me when I was very young, and she who had frolicked naked with me in the playpen, yes ravishing, and I think no longer at rest.

I'll keep you posted on this as I go along.

March 27, 1969

EIGHTEEN LITTLE KIDS, black, five or six years of age, two black unwed mothers, about sixteen, a middle-aged woman teacher, two old, white volunteers, ladies from northwest, paints, tools, colored paper, bulletin boards, a small kitchen, a small yard next to the church, the directress of the Community Center in Anacostia, and me. Such will be the mornings of my life for the next three weeks.

I feel uneasy with blacks all around, and scared when I have to walk around in an all-black neighborhood, so it will be a challenge and I hope fun. I have to wake up extremely early to get there in time, and if I can't find a ride, I will have to bus down there (yes, from up here in white security). Wearing my corduroy jacket and bow tie (I could never get away from that), I felt, to put it mildly, like shit. If only I could look poor. Instead, I look rich and degenerate.

Peter Lee has been very good to me. He has repeatedly told me that I should take all the time I need at the office to write you and reflect or simply relax, and that I should tell him if I feel that I am being used or overused the wrong way.

So I spend lots of time, at least today, reading Lawrence Durrell's *The Black Book*. It is the kind of prose and thoughts I would like to write if I had the time/energy/skill/abandon/inspiration. Very mysterious. He makes you want to meet him there in his midnight dives and make love to his fantastic women and smoke his fantastic hashish. I have digressed, for today I have read and reflected and done little, and I left the church two hours early. Washington is windy and I am calm; Washington is cold and I am warm.

March 28, 1969

TODAY I HAVE roamed the streets of downtown Washington in search of inspiration and probably some beautiful girl. My duties today have been mundane and rather repetitive, so there is little to tell. Only that walking in the full and busy streets is beautiful, and something rediscovered for me. I walk and let my mind roam and begin talking to myself, thinking in fantasies and dreams. For instance, one of my perennial favorites: I'm walking down the streets, a striking

character among the milling minions, and the movie begins
. . . CHARLES TRUEHEART . . . URSULA ANDRESS . . . IN THE JEAN-
LUC GODARD PRODUCTION OF . . . THE SON OF GOD . . . and the
camera does all sorts of neat tricks with instant shots of my
face and then in contrast to all the mediocre people surrounding me on the street, and then back to me as Ursula
runs from a still-moving taxi into my open arms . . . and then
the spell breaks and I have walked into a telephone pole and
I must return to the office because my lunch hour is not two
and a half hours long. But for today, really nothing.

March 30, 1969

EISENHOWER IS DEAD, my first day in Anacostia did not occur,
and by now, lunchtime, everyone has gone home. For today,
there is nothing to report, nothing to think about that is
related to my job. Of course, I am full of other thoughts and
feelings about last weekend, and most of them can best be
expressed by saying that I am young, confused, in love, and
tired.

Once again, I have sat here in the office filing some useless
cards for the fund drive and my mind has been on Jennifer,
the new one with so much charm. I suppose the important
word is confused, because I don't know what to do. I am
swept off my feet every single time, and I do wild things like
this morning, when I drove over to her house at seven-thirty
with a note, one of those ones that ends up ruining everything because it's so sincere, but discovered her mailbox was
too close to the house itself, and not at the end of the driveway as I had thought it would be. So I turned yellow and
drove away and now I am depressed. I prayed this morning

when I first got to church, and now I feel selfish, because I asked for, literally asked for, Jennifer and her affection. I am rapidly going off the deep end.

April 1, 1969

THEY WERE ALL over me, all for the first time different little children with normal Josh-like hang-ups and misbehavior. For the first fifteen minutes, they couldn't get over my smile. I sat at their table at breakfast, with just three little boys, and they sat and ate silently, and six eyes followed my every move. One little girl clung to me for five solid hours, a little brown paw, except around the fingernails and palms, clutched in my white one. I learned later she had no father, no male in the house since she was born, and I was Daddy. I read them all a book and participated in their public speaking session.

"Where do you live?"

"I live at frojfjskksjclsociwht."

"Can you say that a little more clearly so all of us can hear you? Can you take your hand out of your mouth, please? Thank you. Now, what is your address?"

"Frowty-svn chfkkijs larnbd, sofest."

"Good. Now Clarissa, how about you? Can you tell us . . ."

One of the other workers is an unwed mother about sixteen who is black and beautiful and for the first time I considered changing my answer on that sexuality questionnaire. (Would you marry a black?)

I felt, to my surprise, fairly well-integrated in Anacostia. The blacks smiled at me when we passed them on the street. (We went for a walk around the town.) As a matter of fact, the only shit I took all morning was from one of the few whites I saw: a man about sixty with a white-hair crew cut, who stopped and looked at me for a minute, and then proceeded to give me hell about my hair. How I ought to be ashamed of myself and how I ought to wear it like his (rubbing his hand up and down his skull) and how I wouldn't listen, he knew, but that he was telling me right nevertheless. But I was redeemed, in a way, when he said in parting, muttering, that I shouldn't be hanging around with nigras anyway. I said that I guessed he had his problems too, and he stalked off.

Another picture of black Washington. We were walking down the street and a black called out to the head teacher and asked her if she wanted a color TV. She answered Yes, two please, and he said he would put her order in. She could expect it Friday, he said, and they both laughed. I suppose that there will be trouble Friday because it is Martin Luther King Day and also because it is Good Friday and Black Friday. I may not even be able to go back to St. Philip's if they burn down the church, or is it southern whites who burn churches. Or both.

But I have had a satisfying, busy, breakless day, and I am feeling *not* that I am doing anyone a favor, although I probably am, but that I am doing myself a favor, if anyone, and at the very least, that I am seeing something that I have never seen before and that this is perhaps most important for the future. I have almost, in one day, stopped seeing blacks as something different, something to fear. Yesterday I went for a long walk on the canal to mull over my love crisis, which is still unresolved because I am so chicken, and I sat down at the side of the towpath. Halfway through a cigarette, a black emerged from the woods, a fisherman I think, and I immediately started walking back where there were whites. Someday I will get over it, even though they don't want me to. I wish I had my prayer on newness with me. Never before has it seemed so personally appropriate. Groping in the dark for a light switch, which, I should now add, I hope I never find. Help us, dear God, to always scratch the surface.

April 2, 1969

MORE SOUL-SAVING in darkest Anacostia. I helped make Easter baskets for an hour and a half, roughhoused on the church lawn for another hour, and then was too exhausted to do anything more. The kids are great and I feel completely accepted into their world. I learn more about them every day. Often when I feel that one or another of them suddenly shows a spark of intelligence, I immediately pump him for more, and then I am totally disillusioned when he shoves a stick into another child's stomach. I was in charge of all of them when we went outside and believe me it was no easy task. There was at least one crying at every moment. With excruciating patience I would go over and ask him why he did it, as if any child could have given me a straight answer. Constant fighting over Hula Hoops, beach balls, sticks, crying, whining because one boy was rubbing dirt in another's eyes. Noses running, children running down the street in front of speeding trucks, and all, nevertheless, very obedient to me, which is reassuring. I suppose as long as I can take the "Next time you want the Hula Hoop, don't hit Gertrude, just ask her if she wouldn't mind letting you use it when she's done" attitude, which is absurd to begin with because absolutely no child in his right mind would *ever* ask for anything that way, then I guess I'll be okay.

Am also doing much weak bullshit — airport, delivery, errand, mimeo, typing, chatting little — but I am kept busy and still find plenty of time to weep over lost and found loves. I can feel my yellowness fading away, but I feel it will turn to hardened gray apathy rather than burgeoning, flaming passion. I'm having a difficult parental situation, but I get a headache when I think about it, so I will reserve it for an off-the-record letter some other time when I'm feeling more at ease. I am still young.

April 3, 1969

YOUR CALL and I'm plunged into thought, reassured, cared for. I told Jennifer, who was there when you called, all about you, and then we talked about God. I believe in people but not in God, she said, and life is really a joke. I said the first part was God Himself, and the second part was not important, even if it were true; that if you look at it that way, then things aren't worth much so, yes, go ahead and believe in people and you are where it's at. Besides, Jennifer is beautiful and that's enough.

Anacostia and I hide Easter eggs, easily, in the church-yard, and then help the little ones hunt them when they return from a walk to the museum. Little Nathaniel jumps into my arms every morning and we discover together, with hands and fingers and few words, that my hair is long and fair and smooth, and his is very short and jet black and fuzzy, and both are different and both beautiful. He grins and I am swept, as I am often, off my feet by the sheer beauty of his smile. Ronnell has a girl and so do I.

"Does she go to your house?"

"Yes."

"Does yours go to your house?"

"No, but I go to hers and watch TV. Her name is Doris and she is five too."

And fuzzy hair, no doubt.

Larry is over in the corner beating someone up. I lose my patience and go over to tell him that he must stop hitting people for no reason. I shake his tiny ear, and he is suddenly shocked. He spends the rest of the morning quiet, trying to catch my eye to see if I'll smile. I do, winking at him, and suddenly he is happy too. Twenty minutes later he is beating up someone else in the same corner. I walk over and he actually says he's sorry, walking away. We're still friends because he gave me a jelly bean from his basket which I helped him to make.

Talking with the teacher after school: I learn things I never knew; there is so much I have missed living in the suburban ghetto, so much that I thought I never wanted to see. She tells me of Nathaniel's family, ten children and a mother who never even talks to them. There are no chairs in the house to seat the family at dinner, so they all line up against the wall with their plates and slide down to the floor and eat scrunched up in the corner. There is no room there to grow physically so they don't grow emotionally and they are set back. I never, never conceived of anything like that.

Mirrors: most of the kids in Head Start live in homes with only one mirror above the sink, which they are too small to reach. I never realized how important a mirror is, to a child, so that he can feel something about what he is and looks like to others. Children need a feeling of success very early, any kind, a feeling of worth and giving, a self-gift of self-hope and self-love which can come by knowing, even at age five, that they exist, are living beings among other similar-different human beings, and have a reason and a way of living, that they know it and grasp it (as I did and all of us that I know did). But — and this is the incredible thing to learn at my age — they don't. These kids grow up without hope and affection, not knowing whether they will be able to live in a good way — because they probably don't even know what a good life is all about, what love and other people are, because they never had it and chances are their parents didn't either. Fair-haired me can arrive and be happy and kind, even just be a boy-body, and they can show me and *themselves* that they have something which is love.

On an inspiration, I proceeded to the close of the Washington cathedral and found the formidable Jim Anderson, very quiet, extremely interested, and in many ways, like you. The same manner of speech, the same way of making people feel that they are important and that someone cares about them. He had just gotten your letter and recognized my name. I told him (my candor will destroy me someday) almost immediately about my feelings toward Harper, and to my surprise he almost agreed with me. He said he hoped I would tell Harper everything I told him. Harper: urbane, efficient, self-important, kind, struggling, interested, unemotional, responsible. Those are hardly criticisms, and they are not meant to be. It is simply that initial expectations plus previous personal impressions did not jibe with immediate com-

munications and further, deeper impressions. He is always
genuine with me, but often insensitive to what I am feeling.
I think he knows that I would rather be working with services
or discussing worship, as opposed to picking him up at the
airport and delivering letters downtown, but he would be
hard pressed to admit that he knows it. I should not be doing
those things with my time or his, but I would be hard pressed
to tell him for fear that our relationship might be hurt along
with his feelings. He also might be able to shoot me down
pretty quickly. Slow, I think, is the word at St. John's, and
I can see perfectly and exactly why, and that that is right and
good, and I would be a true whippersnapper to try and buck
it. I remain sane because I know that he knows just what I
am feeling, and it may hurt him, but I know he is trying.
I simply feel that a confrontation at this time would hurt us
both, especially him, and I *am* fond of him and respect what
he does with his own time (wakes at five-thirty to work, etc.).
I am too young to ask him to do differently. I am not being a
martyr. I am being absolutely honest with you, and with
myself, though I am always less sure of the latter. My young-
ness (the catchword for my hang-ups during the past two
weeks) will come up later in this message.

A worthwhile digression, now back to Jim Anderson. So
he talked about his job and how he could never hassle work
like Harper's — that's why he got out of the parish ministry.
He said you made a similarly motivated decision in coming
to Exeter. He spoke of the frustrated clergy and also the
Washington diocese as one with the most "ferment" in the
country. The more I hear, the more I'm inclined to believe
him. We reached the subject of his exact job, and how he
was a counselor to various parishes. So it finally got around

to this: A clergyman from a rural Maryland church telephoned Anderson and said he was having trouble with his
church youth group; Anderson promised him he would take
care of it and try to send a young person. Well, who should
pop into his office in the fullness of youth but me, who is
going to Olson, Maryland, Sunday next to "observe" the
proceedings of the meeting of the youth group, take notes,
and then meet privately, without adults, with the youths in
the group. Then, having formulated lucid conclusions about
the problems of the group, and drawn up incisive plans for
the future of the group, I will meet with Anderson and the
clergyman and rap.

And now me. If I could tell you in a word, things are
going too *fast*. Things, and I will use that word until I get to
specifics, go far too quickly for me to even think about them
and be able to decide on them the way I want. Everything
is too easy when you let it go by, but the ease is so un-
satisfying. I suppose I am built so that ideally every thought
that I have should not come unless it is preceded by an
emotional/intellectual trauma. The questions of who am I
and where am I going and even where have I been are on
my mind. Where do I begin? Drawing on just the past
twenty-four hours, I could type for years, and probably will.
Today has been a real mindfuck, and thinking how to communicate it is another one entirely.

Love life: Desperately in love with one girl now, a different
one last week, and another the week before. Still in love with
all three and unable to communicate anything to them,
scared, unsure, and very young. I haven't called Edie or

Alice for over a week and sure enough, both of them have
called me during the typing of this. The triple burden: I love
it. Wanting very much to express my exact feelings to Jennifer, but thinking back on past experiences when I have
pushed things and they haven't worked out, but also thinking
back on times when I said nothing and things died. Deeply
I want affection and I want a chance to give it. I *know* (if
there is anything at all that I know) that I have that affection,
and I am frustrated when I can't find someone to give it to.
A girl. I am grateful that I have plenty of males to give it to
at school, but still, no girl. Edie and Alice both go just so far,
in every sense of the word, and mostly in the area of spiritual
honesty, and then stop. Sex is a big part, but it is not all.
Somewhere here is a plea for advice, but don't feel obligated.
Jennifer is new to me, exciting, unexpected, brilliant, much
poise, much disillusionment. We listened to Dylan last night
as we talked about life, as it happened, and she felt it was a
joke. I don't know how I was heard, but I think my feelings
were as Dylan sang them in the background,

> There are many here among us
> Who think that life is but a joke,
> But you and I we've been through that,
> And this is not our fate.
> So let us not talk falsely now,
> The hour is getting late.

I wish I knew how she felt now about it, but I am too
chicken, and in a way too thoughtful to ask her and find out.
Something is growing between us, but in a word, she would
not groove on the Phillips Church-Love Ag. God, she is so
great I keel over when I think about her. *That* is called youth

and I am glad as hell I am still young. I will never be able to face middle age.

Parents: A big trauma, and I feel badly about it. No communication. I am uneasy, harassed, inconsiderate, and I know they are all those things. Sometimes I feel that living with my family is the most unpleasant thing in the world — fighting, sarcasm, martyrdom, bitterness. I want to tell them all about me; God, I am desperate to tell them, but at the same time I am too tired and too nervous to do so. With you, I feel more confident. I can say things, and you know what I mean, you are younger, you can respond. With them, it would mean not only the explaining (in case I didn't tell you, they don't know, but guess, about CT and grunts) but also the feeling that whenever I left the house, they would be suspicious, which I don't want. But they pump me about it in very subtle ways, and they are desperate to talk to me about it, and I to them, and we sit knowing what's on our minds and talk about nothing. Frustration and youth.

Crux: So things, all these things, plus work and the usual things of life, are all happening and I am standing here. Everything is flying by. I often reach out and try to catch just one thing, as I am trying to do now for you. I try to clutch it, fondle it, keep it with me for a few hours, like during a walk along the canal, but then it escapes, and something new flies into my hand to stay for a short, too short time.

It is a poor metaphor but it is me now, and I am pained because I cannot be more explicit. Jennifer is kind of against smoking. It would mean something to her and to me if I stopped. I decided to last night. This morning I was driving

through downtown traffic, wanted a cigarette, thought one
way, thought another, incredible conflict, thoughts, truths,
lies, all spinning at an amazing rate. What I wanted to do, it
seemed, battled with what I would probably do, which
battled with what I was doing, reaching into the old inside
left coat pocket and shoving in the dashboard lighter. By
four this afternoon I had gone through a pack of haggars. As
the empty package flew into Jim Anderson's trash can, I was
furious with myself, but it had happened. Trivial but it
reflects my thinking, pleasing others versus being honest with
myself versus doing what simply happens, unconsciously.
Versus versus versus versus versus.

"What more can a gentleman say? He can say no more."
                                        — Bertolt Brecht

April 7, 1969

I LEARNED the story of Dr. Harper's old parish this morning
as I drove him out to his country house near Front Royal,
Virginia. I also learned the story of you and him, when you
were almost chosen as his curate. The drive was long and
good because we were able to talk. Our subject matter was
inconsequential, except that we both learned about each
other's pasts, mostly I about his, and I think we came to a
"greater understanding" of each other. So that was my morning with a beautiful drive, and I spent the afternoon delivering lilies to old ladies.

I bought and started *A Rumour of Angels* over the weekend and it looks pretty good. I am still finishing *The Black
Book* and am in the middle of some poems by John Berryman,
which aren't bad. The weekend, which began with an event-

less Friday (my rationale for not writing) even though it was good, was fairly full of traumas. Alice came to see me at church Friday afternoon, and we had one of the most dismal conversations I ever care to remember. I have a feeling that is on the wane. I spent from 11 A.M. Saturday to 3 A.M. Sunday with Jennifer, which was a series of ups and downs, closeness and unsureness, love and anger.

And then Sunday afternoon Edie called and said that she was going crazy. I fretted for three hours after telling her that I would think for a while and then call, and then I went to her house. We had a confessional; things were and are at least honest and definitely uncertain, though we will at least write now, and watch to see how things are in June.

As you can tell, my life is kind of sleeping through a barrage of meteors. I open one eye every once in a while to see, swallow, and digest one chunk of life as it swoops by, bringing light and substance from somewhere else into my blood stream, quickening my pulse so that my eyes are wont to open more and more often: a mixed metaphor. Yes, in a way, life is very much like a mixed metaphor. You might pass that one on to CTH,III.

April 8, 1969

"I HAD LONG talks with Ed Barnes at the end of last term, and we talked a lot about the *persona,* which he described as the shell, that which you project and which is built around what you are inside. And he said that those people with the most *persona* get along best and are the fullest people because the thicker and more invulnerable the shell, the more there is inside you. And I fear for you now, because you seem to me to be one of those lost, sensitive souls in the big city with no *persona,* and that's why you are so somber. You have blown everything, because you think you know who you are, or you think you know that you don't know who you are, and there is nothing left."

I have tried so hard and worked so hard to shed what I was not, and now I find that I am without a face, and I want the old — or anything — back to cover what I most deeply am. I am all heart and all mind and no personality, no gentle blend of human elements to make me a person, to make me the person who is good with other persons, who is like and unlike other persons, but I am now just bare wires. I am there for people to see me as I think I am, and at times as I know I am, and I want them to learn me and love me or learn me and hate me, but to be anything less would be a lie to them and to me. And yet now, I am found wanting in just what I wanted so badly to discard. I am so pure and so real that I am only loving, and unlovable in the sense that I have little substance to coat the skeleton of what I am.

In quotations, Judson M. Phillips to Charles Trueheart, at lunch today. Next, my own reflections on what he told me, to be taken as part of the story, not as crestfallen as it seems, only thoughts and possibilities explored after an illuminating and often shattering conversation with someone whom I respect and like very much, who is at peace with himself and who can afford, both for me and for him, to say what he did.

✿   ✿   ✿

"Are you tired?"

"No, but very boggled in the mind."

"Why?"

"Because it is so exciting to be with you. My day has been very full."

She lowered her head and her hair fell dangling to the side of her face. I didn't see past it, only the long dark hair, and the shape behind it, reacting secretly.

"I took a walk Monday after work because we got off. Down by the canal with Edward, just thinking. Long walks give me time to think about everything that is rushing in at me, all the time."

"What did you think about?"

"Well, as long as I'm being honest, I thought about you. I even wrote you a note which I brought over the next morning but was too scared to give to you."

She paused, tossed her hair, and looked up from the floor. "What did it say?"

"It said just that. That I was thinking about you and that I wanted you to know it. Simply that."

"Mmm."

April 9, 1969

YOUR LETTER PUT me on guard. There are days that strike me as full, and there are days that strike me as empty. So when I say I am not feeling much, then I suppose I should say that I am feeling a great deal of emptiness or lethargy or indifference or what have you, but they mean the same thing. Today, in many ways, has been one of those nothing days, one of those days when the most exciting thing I do is write this letter, though it is often empty too, and probably should be. I am not about to write down three pages of bullshit when I have nothing to say. I hope you can accept that.

JCH, like all humans, has good times and bad times. When we are alone for long periods of time, he becomes warmer and more open about his past. The drive out to his place in Virginia, for instance, was fun because we both talked about our pasts, and we were willing to be honest. However, when I say that I don't think he has much empathy for my job, and bear me out on this, I mean that the demands he makes are either insensitive or carefully calculated to make me labor. I do not feel more alone than ever when I have contact with him. I simply realize that every time I talk to him that I must ready myself for his tone and style and mentality. Maybe, and I too am fishing, he is not insensitive, but *a*sensitive. That, as far as I know, is a new word. However, it is hard to believe that someone who would ask me to wash his car as part of an internship in the church and in theology is really understanding why I'm here and why he took me on.

I'm sorry that Peter wouldn't show you my letter. I forget the contents, and maybe he's right, but as far as I know, there's nothing in it that you shouldn't see. It's probably that I was rapping about grunts or something and they didn't want to hurt your virgin ears.

I had a good long talk with Mama and Papa on Monday night and we have been more pleasant since. I began by telling them that living at home was one of the most un-pleasant experiences of the last four years and we took it from there. Last night was Mama's birthday so things were pleasant then. I think your advice is probably the soundest yet, and though I can't express it quite correctly, telling them

one important thing each day is a fantastic idea. I'm not
getting through because I am low now, but believe me it was
a potent suggestion. My wrath is vented, I hope we understand each other better now. I must clear up one more thing.
My letter yesterday and I'm sure many others have sounded
pretty desperate. I think you know me well enough to
realize that I like to pour out shit like that just so I can get
pity. The problems are very real for me, but I am able to
cope with them much of the time, no matter what they are.
The things that I was communicating yesterday were things
that bothered me at lunch, and for a while afterward, and at
certain very intense moments over the weekend. They have
come up before, but I write them down to clarify them in my
own mind, and because they were particularly evident and
present when I wrote them down and before. You need
send no ambulance. I am, I think, sane.

There is little more to say about today, except that Zeke
and I ate on the lawn in seventy degrees and watched the
pretty girls walk by. Who, at that moment, was sitting in a
12:05 class? Poor devils. A roast beef on a hard roll with
mustard and a large Coke is different from the dining hall.
We suddenly realized how unreal it was that we were both
sitting there. We took possession of the situation and began
to roll around laughing in the sun, getting the sun in our hair.
Talk about communion.

April 10, 1969

School drifts away like a part of my past, and when I see
Zeke, I grope for some remnant of what was. I try to remember how I hated Pubes or how I felt when I got out of

bed for morning chapel, and I am surprised how little I remember, and almost exclusively so when it comes to feelings. The heart has no memory, the head no smiles or tears. I hope I coined that. It is pretty brilliant, especially the first part.

April 14/15, 1969

I WROTE TWO PAGES this afternoon and for the first time destroyed them because they were representative of a momentary state of disgust which I hope has gone by now, after the kickoff of the Three-Year Program for St. John's, a gala dinner at the Statler Hilton. I have been busy, and also busy-busy, and that is why I was unable to write yesterday. I might have been able to last night, but I made a situational decision to do otherwise, to escape, all motivated by disgust at the fact that I had not been able to write. A vicious circle indeed. Confession: in fact, sir, I had been trying, in my recent vicious response to you, to go beyond the defensive to the offensive. But that is past. Your response heartened me. Forgive me.

Yesterday I returned from a fairly routine morning at Head Start only to find that instead of being able to talk to Mr. Lee, as I had planned, and to Anderson, as I had planned and eventually did, I had to drive through the traffic to the main post office to mail leaflets *and* go out to buy a tire for JCH's car, which took me until four-thirty. So, I find myself feeling two things. First, action: Today, and I hope tomorrow, I talked and will talk to Lee about the whole thing. Today he dropped a few hints that he knew what was up and what I was feeling, and we talked for a few minutes about it. I told him that I was going to stop at St. Philip's at the end of the week so as to be able to read, write, and call more, and he was glad to know that I was honest enough to begin to say what I felt about what I was doing.

He is extremely warm and I would really like to get to know him better. Besides, his wife is a real doll, and I am attracted to her, I think even more than physically, which is of course pretty reasonable considering everything. (Little insight into the dream world of Charles No Middle Initial Trueheart, much?) Anyway, I hope to accomplish something in that vein tomorrow.

My second reaction is a new one, that of a budding understanding of JCH. I noticed when he asked me about the tire yesterday that he was almost embarrassed to do so, and that he even offered a little apology about asking me. ("I know this has nothing to do with the ministry, but it may teach you how to buy a tire.") I am fond of him, and he *is* kind, and I think you would be mistaken not to ask him back to school only because of what I say. Today, under a few crossed signals, I took his car home to get changed for the dinner, and he found himself without one and had to walk from the church all the way home. When I went to pick him up he was extremely nice, and we are greater friends than ever. I think he suffers from a profound compulsion to assert himself while not really wanting to do so, and I super-identify with that. I will probably emanate a little JCH when I am older, if not now. This is not self-berating, because (and this is not one of those cliché only-word-to-use situations) I have a profound respect for him and will do my best to tell him everything I can.

✿   ✿   ✿

One snatch of Miss Edie which I now remember and thought you might like: "If I could have three solid private hours with Mr. Gleason I would have myself solved for years." Voilà. ESG lives.

Let me try to summarize my weekend. I spent Friday and Saturday evenings with Jennifer and I think we might make it. I have taken the painful approach of a buddy, asexual and witty, and she is beginning to see that it is indeed an approach, an attempt at a rapprochement, and understands that I would rather be serious and in love but that I am giving a little for her. We are, to my amazement, much closer in the sense that I have never known, except for perhaps my pre–Fall Dance days with Edie. See letter to CTH,III for an explanation of that feeling; you have my permission if you need it.

Meat: Olson, Maryland, Sunday night, and I found myself in a situation that I would never have imagined.

The clergyman, Roger Simpson, late in getting into the ministry, about 45, very ineffectual and devoted, an unfortunate combination in the light of his problems with a group (there were only five Sunday, all males) of youths in the Senior Youth Group. Such students I never imagined existed — short hair, from my standpoint immature, and with little or no respect for poor Mr. Simpson.

The first part of the discussion centered on a trip they were planning, and they showed little originality or drive to get it going. Simpson told me this was his biggest problem: they had no initiative or confidence to present an idea and carry it through. They could *do* things when they were instructed but could not create. This was evident. It suddenly occurs to me that that is one of the things an Exeter education can do for someone, to give him the power to originate, create, organize, and overcome problems — to defend and argue a conviction. These guys had none of that. So there was a drawback from their point of view, and as an observer (you can't imagine, and neither can I, their reaction to me, with my radically different appearance, age, and general air of savoir faire — blowing smoke rings with a suaveness never even conceived in the Williams House Butt Room — sent to "observe" a man thirty years my senior). I saw that part of it. But I was most disturbed by the fact that Simpson was doing it wrong. As I told Anderson yesterday when I went for another exciting visit to the cathedral — Anderson is exciting to talk to, and utterly with it and with everything I was not only saying but thinking and feeling — Simpson has taken the wrong approach, and I reacted wrong. My reaction was to want to take the entire group under my wing and do it "right."

Of course, as I realized driving home, that was neither what I was sent to do or what I should do. My purpose was to help Simpson. But it was a little late, because at the end of his meeting I asked him (guilt: was I rude?) to leave. When he went out, I asked the members of the group to meet with me the following week, to bring more people, especially girls, and to bring something short "which you have read that you either enjoyed or that meant something to you, and we will consider it in terms of a prayer."

This is what I didn't like about Simpson's approach: first, he, as an individual, was reacting to them wrong. He told me privately he didn't want to be a "father" to them. How-

ever, he went the other way and tried to be one of the guys
and this evidently and embarrassingly turned them off completely. They made fun of him, interrupted him, joked about
what he was saying. Two of them whispered to each other
the whole time he was talking. Admittedly, he should not be
a father to them. I doubt if he could even do that. But he
should find a new line and talk to them from a different, but
understanding, level. Second, the topic they were discussing
for forty-five minutes was prayer and worship. This topic
turned them off, and I saw why. If only they could be given
the notion that prayer and worship are part of "normal everyday life." Next Sunday I am going to begin by asking them
to rap about themselves and then talk about "normal everyday life." That's why I asked them to bring something to
read: to see if whatever it is they like is something like "faith"
and whether that has anything to do with "God" or whatever.
What do you think? Their lives are fairly unsophisticated,
and secluded (I doubt if many have lived anywhere outside
of Olson) and I have to begin at the beginning, something
Simpson has failed to do. I think they see a little connection
between life and God, and we shall see, heh-heh, if there is
any. Nevertheless, I think Anderson was impressed and only
reminded me that Simpson was the central issue, that we
were not trying to see which of Simpson and Trueheart is a
better teacher. I must keep that in mind every second next
Sunday. If it goes longer than three minutes, I hope to talk
about their gripes about Simpson so I can better see their
bag, with which bag I am not familiar. So that was Sunday
night, and that was my talk with Anderson. I hope he in-
vites me out for some intensive rapping soon. I know he is
busy.

Whatever the case, on the way back (long drive) I had
that same catharsis-mindfuck that comes after such situations. So many insights and feelings and inability to express
or even register them. I talked to myself the whole way
back. If the steering wheel could learn, it would be brilliant.
"Oh gosh," Donovan says, "life is really too much."

*   *   *

Anacostia has been more of the same. Extremely tiring,
and I am exhausted by 11 A.M. The kids, I fear, are losing
some of the novelty of my newness. They keep saying things
like "Duke could really lick you." Imagine my predicament
at being put down by the memory of a St. Paul's man who
worked at Head Start last term on his project, and left to go
play *lacrosse*, no less.

One of the black girls who works there (about my age,
very attractive) and I took all the kids to the playground at
the Anacostia Elementary School Monday morning. Parked
on the street was a truckful of black guys who started swear-
ing at her ("Gonna do the trick with the Whitey?" "Too good
for us?" "White cunt") and giving her a really hard time.
She got really pissed off and eloquently told them to go jam
it up their simple black asses. I asked her rather innocently
afterward if they had been giving her a hard time because of
me and she said, "No, they're young and simple." And a big
smile; and again I kicked myself for having checked the
wrong box on the questionnaire.

April 16, 1969

IMAGINE A MAN who is the essence of realism and you have
Peter James Lee, whom I am now convinced should be at

school at some point next year for a stay longer than a church
service, but including one. Spiritual realism is his bag and
he is brilliant.

I went in to see him just an hour ago after returning from
Anacostia, which was very tiring and uneventful. I shot my
wad to his calm countenance, which had been thinking the
same things about me and, as it turned out, about himself.
I told him that if possible, I would like to stay away from
the mimeograph machine (a clever symbol representing all
that is busywork) and that I would like to call with Colmore
as often as I can. As a result, he said that he understood,
realized, apologized: "We have been using your body more
than your mind. You have become an errand boy in the
worst way, and I'm glad you have seen perhaps the most
tragic thing about the ministry, and the frustration that
results from it." And taught: "But it is a good thing to see it,
as you have so fully, and often I feel the same way. I come
home from a day at seven-thirty and realize 'My Lord, I have
accomplished nothing. Is this what I've given my whole life
for?' The thing I'm so glad to see is that first you've realized
it early in the game, and that second, you've decided to do
it, to try to understand it and overcome it without either
resigning yourself to it or completely ignoring it. You have
already left an indelible impression on all of us, that you are
bright, willing to work, candid, and sensitive. I can tell you
honestly that you are very well liked, even by the old ladies,
which is an incredible thing for a lot of them who live only by
distant impressions and *U.S. News and World Report*." He
concluded by saying that he would not promise to keep me
away from the mimeograph machine, and as a matter of fact,
I would still be at the mimeograph machine, but that he

would try hard. I was to keep pushing him to do so, to keep me doing more important things.

Such as for starters: attending a seminar at Virginia Seminary next Monday with eight seminarians, a theologian, himself, and a lay parishioner from another church. I spoke to Colmore, and he said he rarely plans a day or knows what he is going to do, but that he would take me whenever possible when he went out. PJL and I are going to talk to Shands and Hawkins next week. We are going to work out a program of noonday services made up mostly of movies and speakers on the topic of urban/racial/youth problems, and I have been given the task of selecting the flicks to be used. So from what we have as intentions, I am ecstatic. I hope we can carry them through.

As I left, he put his hand on my back and said that we should talk every day. I like him very much, and the temporary leer for his wife is fading away.

April 17/18, 1969

MY EVENING of the seventeenth, despite my fatigue, was a charming and sophisticated one as I might have expected in the home of JCH. He was relaxed and I was relaxed and tired. The evening was full of bubbling, if uninspiring, conversation. We discussed Paris, and mutual friends, and various trivialities that made me feel good. I felt close and sympathetic (from my perch of grandeur) toward the rector. As I get to know him, I feel much closer and begin to regret my jumped-to conclusions about him at the beginning. I don't really regret them, but I can see them in perspective, and realize that he has to do much of what he hates in his business (and it is business) situation.

Today I attended the monthly meeting of the downtown episcopal convocation. Lots of old ladies and paranoid clergymen discussing absolutely nothing, most of them either feeling a great sense of importance or, for Harper, Colmore, and Trueheart of St. John's, cynicism. The topics, which I have forgotten, were pretty trivial. Twenty minutes into the meeting I was surprised to hear Harper and Colmore coming out with the funniest comments about the meeting, under their breaths, that I have heard them utter about anything. About ten minutes were spent discussing the location of the next meeting, which turned out to be St. John's, and the date, all the ladies throwing in their two cents about why this or that should be the date. One clergyman kept chirping on about how his church was so destitute compared to St. John's. Colmore said on the way back that he was the type that "turns me into a raving son of a bitch in four seconds." Colmore asked Harper afterward who would represent St. John's at the next meeting. Harper started to say something about a rotating basis, and Colmore said, "You mean who-ever's on the shit list that morning?" When Colmore referred to one of the ministers there as a "fink," Harper asked him what that meant. Colmore answered, "Well, asshole."

I guess the old ladies involved feel that they're doing some-thing worthwhile, and it gives them a little something to be proud of and to do besides watch TV. That's typical of the conflict that the church is in, a lot of crap that is so necessary for some people.

So that is all. I have finished with St. Philip's and will

return to the church next Monday, having been bestowed
the honor of being crossbearer on Sunday. It seems I will be
the first member of my family to do so other than spiritually.
Quite symbolic, if you stop to think about it.

This epistle to St. Edward has been too whimsical, but.

April 21, 1969

I WAS THE first to arrive last night, having sped from northwest Washington, down Suitland Parkway, having stopped
at a Hot Shoppes Junior and completely wrecked what was
left of my stomach on black coffee and french fries, arriving
in Olson at six-thirty with a half-hour wait and the first guy
not arriving until seven.

They filtered in, and gave me a quick, ashamed look and
then sat down on the chairs and looked at each other,
periodically glancing in my direction, wondering what the
hell was going to happen. "This is ridiculous," I heard someone say in the hall before he came in, and everyone in the
room laughed embarrassedly. By seven-fifteen there were
four girls and eight guys, all the same ones who had been
there last week and more, all staring at me — me continuing
to puff on the ephemeral, cancerous haggar with a grace and
a nervousness unimaginable.

My countenance was cool; however, my outward appearance betrayed the very emotions which had catapulted me
into a state of high tension. Anyway, I sort of chatted with a
few of them about college — what else — and they talked
among themselves about football until about seven-twenty,
when I sent one guy to get the Cokes and began by rapping
about myself and why I was there. One girl raised her hand

and asked how old I was. Seizing the opportunity, I said, "How old do you think I am?" and she said she didn't know. All twelve of them then went around and guessed. Imagine, dear Reverend, my surprise and ego-boostment when the low guess was nineteen, the high guess twenty-five. So we were off to a good start. I told them I was seventeen, waiting to hear from college just like them. ("Which ones?" "Harvard, Amherst, and Johns Hopkins." Oh, swoon, swoon.) A couple of the girls were especially astonished to discover my true age, and I imagine they were snowed, but I could hardly let matters such as the aforesaid interfere with the course of my endeavor. So I continued to rap, and then let each of them rap (*told* each of them to rap) about themselves, which in some cases turned out to be pretty valuable. (One guy's father had been a truck driver and they had moved all over the country living in trailer camps. His father drowned while scuba diving in 1964, and his mother then married a man to whom she was introduced by the son himself. He's interested in aviation . . .)

That lasted until about ten of eight, at which time I read some things out of *Noonmark* magazine, a brilliant suggestion of Jennifer's — they would feel free to criticize since it was written by people their own age. I read them the quasi-Christian potpourri of Biblical undertones written by Don Buswell, which to learned Biblical scholars like these kids seemed awfully mixed up. (Why baptism after communion? Why does he crawl like a snake along the beach when he has just taken communion?) I think this served to show the ignorance of Exeter English students more than anything else. I felt better when at the reading — not without some undue emotion and vocal quavering — of "Crossings," my own short story in *Noonmark*, they reacted with more sanity. Many said they could identify with the feelings of the author. I asked them to guess what had happened before and what happened after the incident in the story and they were remarkably accurate in their pronouncements. One girl spoke the truth: "They both leave each other bitter, but I sense a loneliness too, which could only have been helped by their being together again. I think there's hope at the end." Indeed, I told them the two of them continued. They were pleased that I told them who wrote it, and that they were part of something in my life now. I could be a human and not just a teacher, as I was for most of the evening.

We discussed the two stories until a little after eight, and then I said it's Roger Simpson time. The ensuing conversation often wandered, but their ability to stay on the subject really amazed me, because whenever someone started to talk nonsense, someone else would jump on him and say he was wasting time and we have to help Charlie so he can tell Mr. Simpson. Undying enthusiasm. I was pleased almost to tears at points when they could not raise their hands high enough or their voices either and I had to actually quiet them down.

"Why was there so much silence when I was here last week?"

"Well, it's not his age, but we just can't talk to him the way we can to you."

"Oh no, you've got to tell him exactly what's on your mind, what's wrong, tell him you think every meeting eats shit. He wants you to say something, and won't mind anything you say as long as you can tell him why."

They were reluctant, but what was most incredible was that they realized much more than I thought about Simpson and his attempts. They said he was a great guy: "It's just that we can't get anything done. We just come here and talk about the football team and he gets mad." They did note one problem of his: "Sometimes he puts the damper on an idea because some people in the group don't like it."

"So he likes you to suggest things and get things done, but only if they appeal to everyone. He's trying to please everyone and ends up pleasing no one?"

"Right."

So the outcome of the evening was mostly that it was their own fault, and that they would have to try a lot harder in the future to get things done. They asked me to come back one more time because they'd had such a good time, but I told them that it was Simpson's show, and their show to help him out as much as they could. I said I would like to come back but I couldn't. I was about to burst with whatever it is one bursts with when one feels boundlessly proud and satisfied. I ended by reading one of my favorite passages from John Barth, and indeed from literature.

Then I left and sang a blues song, composed as I drove along the Beltway, complete with movements, chorus, lyrics, all the way home. The song included the famous "Ours is not to reason why . . ." movement, which is eight minutes long, the perennially inspiring finale with lyrics borrowed from Bob Dylan, and assorted *baby*'s, *sweet honey chile*'s and *tell me now*'s. A moment of true joy and I think, if I understand the word, a time of grace.

Weekend: Friday a swirling time with Jennifer seeing *Romeo and Juliet* after dining at Martin's in Georgetown. Rather a good flick, and I was in semi-tears at the end. I was almost fortunate to see her in tears too, but she hides too much and they would not roll. But she was moved and our palms together were sweaty and warm. We uttered not a word from Connecticut Avenue to Canal Road, and then she said that in the front of some editions of Shakespeare they spend pages and pages trying to prove that Shakespeare didn't really exist. I said, "It's like Jesus Christ; it doesn't matter if he did or didn't." Maybe profound.

Something else which sprang up in the Beltway Blues, another profundity: It is easier to see another man's ass than it is to see your own.

Maybe CTH,III would like that.

As I REVIEW the events of the past forty-eight hours in my mind, I am left with a continuing sense of frustration. Anger, resentment, depression, none of these are a part of my mood yesterday and today. Merely frustration that I, as someone who even modestly believes that he has something to offer, something very different and very alive, something even unique, was not able to project it, to express it, to *be* it for a group of men faced with a difficult task of judgment. I realize the dilemma they, as judges and decision-makers, are in, but I think I am able, if anyone is, to come across as what I am both genuinely, and particularly in this case, quickly, in terms of words and time. So to hear that they were not struck by what I am as something which they wanted leaves me shocked at first, but then really and deeply frustrated at my own lack of articulation — that my desire to give was as

strong as my desire to receive and that the means and subject
of my gift were not seen leaves me sad, and without being
falsely altruistic, sad for them too. But it is done, and I
suppose ours is not to reason why. I am told constantly that
I will emerge all the stronger, and that the defeats will teach
me far more effectively than the successes, which may have
been too plentiful and too quick for my own well-being. By
not being able to spend the next four years attending
Harvard College with some forty Exonians, I may see new
people and things and learn much, especially if I end up at
Johns Hopkins, where I fear I will be very alone, very much
challenged by an entirely new beginning.

That *is* fear, but I think it is good fear, because fear has
been such a small part of my life. I have needed and almost
always received the security of friends, and the assurance of
a future life with a great deal of sameness, and the idea that
I will lose that sameness makes me feel first very afraid, and
then very intrigued at how I will function.

It took me about fifteen minutes to have the entire mass of
expectations and confidence tumble down on top of me, and
know that I will not be living with the people I thought I
would (i.e., you) — perhaps even be far enough away that I
would never see them again. I truly hope that it is not weak
to feel this way, to feel this loss, but I think that the loss is
now a reality, and not a dim apprehension, that the most
important things that I have possessed at Exeter in four years,
the people, will either be far or inaccessible. One of my
ladies told me that if I felt strongly about someone, so
strongly, that I would always be able to see them. But here is
a problem, first of geography, and then of life-style. I can see
myself losing the motive to go and find an old friend, and

thinking that he means less and less to me, but knowing that at one point I never wanted to leave him, and now it has happened, and what we had is permanently gone. That is the only way that sadness enters into my feelings and now that I am thinking about it, sadness is very real.

As I said, the loss is both mine and theirs, but it will be gone, this whole feeling of loss, and the only way I will even remember feeling it so strongly, perhaps, is by rereading this. And then I will chuckle and say that I can't imagine it being so important to me now that I have done this or that and found that better. But I hope I can remember too the reality and strength of my four years at school and remember them as four magnificent years of my life, years of learning and forming a style of life that I suppose will always remain with me in some small way. I am told to be hopeful and think of fresh starts, and it is both easy and hard: easy because I am naturally optimistic about anything I want to do, hard because I will always remember the things about which I was so optimistic in the past. I will live, and I know I will live happily no matter what, but let me never forget that I was sad once, and that my sadness was as strong as any happiness I have ever felt.

April 22, 1969

A MIXED, HANGOVER DAY, with dim memories of terrifying thoughts (and I write this only minutes after the page, undated, that I have enclosed) which leaked almost imperceptibly into two otherwise describable situations. I attended a seminar at Virginia Seminary yesterday between three and

six at which ten rather bland young seminarians discussed
their work projects in various Washington area churches.
A heated argument over Sunday school, in which I interjected some rather pithy comments despite my tendency to
mentally and spiritually wander miles away to Baltimore,
western Massachusetts, Cambridge, and Exeter.

I left the seminar and drove to see and be with a comforter,
Miss Jennifer, whom I had worried about twenty-four hours
earlier. Perhaps it was good that I did, because I am as
convinced of her brilliance as I am, forgive me, of mine.
Seeing her walking down the street from her bus, huge load
of books, hair dangling on the sides of her head, swerving and
stopping on the curb, reaching my arm out to hers and both
of us not talking, merely staring forlorn, she quizzical because
she didn't know about me, and me sympathetic because I
knew about her — no's from Penn, Yale, Radcliffe, Stanford
and Carleton. We touched momentarily before she pulled
away. I saw her pain and felt mine, but she was very good
to me, forgot herself, maybe even really forgot herself and
said that they didn't know what they were doing, and maybe
I even forgot about me when I said the same to her about
her. We left the same — another incident, a ripple or a wave,
or both — and set about starting over and knowing that we
would have to try hard. She and I so seemingly independent,
I knowing that I was not and needing her and everyone so
much, and she not revealing any of this. I selfishly hoped
that she felt it too, and wished that she would express it in
this a time of great need and whatever for others. But that
was too much to ask, and my continuing wishes still continuing, my strength growing, I think, with every small

defeat, my cynicism trying so hard to emerge, and my whatever not letting it, telling myself never to let it take over
completely.

Last night, I forgot to tell you, I went out to a poetry
reading at the Library of Congress, and while I was gone,
JCH came by the house and left me a note:

> CHARLIE: Sorry to miss you. Stopped by to be sure you're still
> in the land of the living. Cheer up — you've got *a lot* going for
> you, including some friends at St. J's — and me.   JCH

I was touched, moved, even catapulted with a warmth
toward this incredibly, beautifully tragic man, who has
helped me in every way through this, whom I will never
forget.

April 24, 1969

THE ASSEMBLY AT Episcopal High tomorrow was called off.
Instead, I will speak Wednesday, so that is off my mind. The
college sweat is off because I am sitting back after a terrible
fight with my father over me manipulating people so that I
could get into college. I am hoping of course for Amherst.
As Peter may have told you, he went to see the principal who
is going to call some people about me. (For which I am
touched. It's that way between Peter and me: no expression,
but a subtle and very strong love that only emerges in acts of
concern like that. Perhaps that's the way it should be, but I
am impatient and it takes so long. I guess that's my real
problem, impatience and youth.) Jonathan Moore has al-

ready called Amherst so I am still hoping. That's what's so shitty about this whole deal, too many friendships put on the line, at stake in something so base as "getting in."

But I didn't write yesterday, and that in itself is symptomatic of my whole condition. I should be writing so that I can say why I am not, but the not is an expression itself. I am feeling very tired and fewer things are seeming exciting. I was not even nervous about the speech, simply bothered by it, by the whole idea of having to do it. *La léthargie* is setting in as it always does toward the end, but not the immediate end, of any delineated period of time, such as my project in Washington. About Wednesday I should have come out of it, like clockwork, like terms' ends. And I don't want to write even when it was so important to me only last week, so forgive me.

April 25, 1969

LAST NIGHT: dinner (what sacrifice!) with my aunt, grandmother, both parents, and little brother, friendly, warm, sparkling.

Heard various rumors about another drug bust at school and shudder at the thought of coming back to the same old drug-fear-rumor atmosphere. Tell me it's not true. Also heard from Jud Phillips that Harvard had only taken twenty-two — at first I was mad but then realized that in terms of Harvard's benefit, they couldn't have made a better decision. Why 1969? Hope to hear soon about your conversation with the admissions officer, especially if he had anything interesting to say about why.

Went to see Jennifer. We were both (when together) talking about college and I am waxing ill of the whole subject. I'm back to my old ultimately destructive self-confidence, back to spending my time worrying about her and everyone else. She told me the truth, that I take things too seriously. I realize it but I live on seriousness and worrying all the time, so I told her maybe now that everything is more or less over in terms of responsibility (will it ever be?) that I may relax for a while. She was happy. I guess.

Then home and a talk until two with my mother for the first time in a while, about love life and my serious-worrying nature. Very enlightening, but she was surprised about my feelings toward deep commitments with girls at such an "early" age. She said early romances never work out, so I told her about Ted Gleason meeting his wife-to-be at age fourteen. She said that's rare, and I guess it is except it's nice to be rare. So I talked myself dry about all my worries. I wish my father hadn't been upstairs asleep because it will be a long time before I can do that again. It's very tough, life and all. One learns to live.

A good conversation with Mr. Lee this morning. Part of it was about what I'm going to do with all this daily written bullshit in terms of St. John's. I think I'm going to let him (Lee) read it early next week and among other things we will decide whether JCH should see it. It's even hard to show Lee all this, and right this second I'm acutely conscious that he will be reading all of this soon and I hope I'm not being uncandid or whatever. Hello, Mr. Lee, you're reaching the end soon. But we spent the morning together talking; I feel closer and very ready to share all of this with him. Mr. Willy Hills was in town today. He came by St. John's and we rapped for a while about what I would be doing. He seems extremely lackadaisical about the whole thing, sort of a let-it-ride attitude, which turns me off in a way.

I can't tell you how different my frame of mind is now that I know someone else will see this. I hope not harmful.

I am feeling very badly about the past few missives. I wish I could be as excited as I was at the beginning but it is all wearing off. The time when I could have described my conversation with Lee in vivid, novelistic detail and style seems to have gone very quickly. Now I feel like I am making an efficiency report of all my activities without much thought or reflection. But if that is the way I am now, and here, then I had better be straightforward about it and not try to write some painful, drudging story that has no meaning for me. I think I tried to explain my lethargy in yesterday's thing. Maybe I have reached a stage of spontaneous and inflexible conclusion, a time when it is my instinct to feel that all is over, that I will learn little more, that I am eager to move on, that I have made the insights and conclusions before and it would be too much trouble to think about others or about rethinking the old ones in terms of whatever happened on a given day. Very typical of me, latching on to the first and most viable conclusion about an experience or thought and then closing myself off to any others that may come up because I am confident that my original one is correct, or should I say "correct"?

Remember that I am trying very hard, and that with plans to make for spring, summer, and fall, the family and home gone very soon from the United States, the plans for college, I have been ignoring my purpose here. It is natural, I think, to do so.

After about three weeks of abstention for some reason, I feel like turning on sometime soon, just as a variety and a little escape from my worries, and as a little rest from twenty-four hours a day of emotional turmoil and painful introspection. Maybe Saturday night will be a good time, but it has reached a point, I think, where I will slowly go off the grunts and seldom return. That is good, because it was only at the beginning of this vacation that I realized that I felt no better after having been zonked, none of my worries were gone, and my subsequent lethargy did little to help me cope with those worries. I think it has something to do with living in a less strained-restrained environment, something to do with the fact that Jennifer is pretty much straight, and I revolve, always, around the current woman.

I hope the return to school will be a pleasant one in those terms, because I don't want to see myself falling into the old pattern of yore. Imagine. This is the first time I have thought about the whole subject of drugs in weeks, except for the hint of probing by the parents, which is becoming harder and harder to avoid. Should they know?

April 28, 1969

NOT UNTIL YOU are pushed into expression, convincing expression, do you actually know and believe what you are thinking; not until you must communicate do you have to express your beliefs realistically, instead of in unchallenged dreams that run through your mind.

A conversation that began with the question of why the blue lights on the field at Dulles Airport (Jennifer and I were there Friday night) blink at a distance and not close up, a mere conversation prompter, grew magnificently, spiritually, into a true feeling of excitement and faith. Yes, she said, the lights were a lot like people. I can't remember whether the point was that as they were actually blinking, to see them too close was not to see them as they really were, because your eyes made more of them than what was there, which sort of stung me; or that people, like lights, were more full, yet always deceiving, but still more full, when they were closer.

It was long ago that this happened, like four days, so I can only remember snatches of it. Somehow we got to talking about a higher being, and I had to explain myself on that one, and then she started pushing me to talk about the church, which I did after much catharsis. The conclusions I came to ended up with her more convinced than I about what I was saying, that people came to church in the hope, every week, that their existence might be given some meaning, some purpose, and the mere fact of their not quite ever reaching it, of finding that meaning, made them continue to leave in hope, and in search of the good in their lives. A startling revelation to me even as it tripped so fluently off my tongue, a shocking realization that I had found out at least why many people (I shy away now from saying *I*) go to church.

The conversation was studded with as many spiritual gems as you can imagine, including one magnificent part when she was criticizing the church as a conscious, structured attempt to be with, close to, related with, others — the fact of premeditatedly celebrating life. I said yes, but at least everyone is close to your own wavelength at a worship service; everyone, though consciously, is celebrating or sharing something. She said, even after I had assured her that it didn't have to happen in church on Sunday, that if anything the joy or sor-

row of sharing should come personally, and after the point of
celebration. She told me a swirling story of herself and two
friends having what I deciphered to be a reasonable facsimile
to our own mindfuck: They were laughing together and
someone suddenly said, "Don't you just love us?" When she
told me I jumped in the air. I said, not unlike a Catholic
missionary happening upon one of his subjects reading the
Bible in the woods for the first time, that yes, that was exactly
it, those are the most religious moments, that was what I
meant by religion or faith or worship or any other name you
might want to tag on it. So we shook on it (touching) and
drove away from the blue lights and our plainly inspiring
worship service, just completed in the road ("Why don't we
do it in the road?") in front of the enormous terminal building, which is not far from being a church — what with a
rather transitory congregation of people meeting old friends
and mothers and soldiers and children and lovers, all of
whom either rise into the sky or descend from it for a brief
jaunt into a new place with new people. My imagination can
run wild on such occasions, but the evening was not over.

   We discussed fate on the way back in the car, and worked
out a way to prove that man has absolute control over his
destiny: Build a vehicle that can go faster than the speed of
light, get in it, and travel an hour ahead of time (this is
theoretically possible) and see what you see. If it looks the
same, only an hour later, then we are pretty much helpless
creatures and the existence of God is scientifically proved
(something I never doubted other than scientifically); *however*, if there is nothing there an hour later (imagine our
conversation about what that nothing would look like) then

we are pretty much in the driver's seat of our own lives, free
to do our own thing.

The evening climaxed (don't hold your breath) with an
argument with her father over man and war, which began
with his rather startling pronouncement that the basis of all
religions is conversion, and that their survival depends on
their ability and capacity to convert people. Believers are
intolerant of nonbelievers and feel more assured if they are
backed by millions of people and never challenged. (I could
say the same thing for the United States of America.) My
religious history was mighty meager, but I fought my way
through that one, hoping the whole time that some clergyman
would descend from above and help my battle against his
point of view. If he's right, then I will be badly shaken,
although oddly enough, it was incredibly satisfying to have
convinced Jennifer that God and faith were not entirely
absurd. Oh, potential hypocrisy, get thee away.

Succumbed to the urges of my generation's sin Saturday
night, and regretted the lethargic hangover Sunday, during
which time I lay around (while not at church, at which place
I read the lesson, good experience) feeling rather sick, having
seen the departure of one grandmother the day before and
expecting the arrival of the other yesterday afternoon. You
know.

May 1, 1969

I HAVE BEEN MOVED in the last three days by both affection
and respect which in some cases I hardly deserved. I leave
St. John's Church and Washington tomorrow with sadness

but a renewed excitement that I have made friends with at least two people for whose friendship I am grateful. These words are flat because they are so simple and so true, but they must emerge this way because I am so moved. To begin with, simply to make it clear for me, I have great affection for John Harper and Peter Lee, and I am boundlessly happy to have theirs.

Tuesday I went to visit St. Mark's, home of Hawkins and Oliver, and they were kind, partially open, and very informative. Hawkins was maybe concerned about his work, kind of a swagger stick sort of person, but casual, sort of a fun, crooked, swagger stick. His assistant, Oliver, was at times very nice and open, at other times rather snide, self-important, and willing to tell just so much. Both of them together are probably good for the church, but they struck me with that very uneasy feeling that they had a big secret, the two of them; that they had and knew a lot, and they were doing good things and there you are, Exeter, and we're glad you came by but don't expect us to tell you everything because we've sweated to be where we are. Nevertheless I learned, and in fairness I think they were glad to talk to me, and I was impressed, indeed, with what I could glimpse of what they were doing. My impressions of people become distorted by time, reflective cynicism (an attitude closely related to cynical reflection) and the words of others — and you will hear the words of others soon.

GOD HELP ME TO FORGET THE WOMAN IN BOSTON WHO MAY READ THIS AMEN

The Episcopal High School experience was a good one. The place is closed from the world, the real world, and I knew then that Exeter was not. There is a wall, much grass and many trees and many Southern students, bright, brighter than I thought. There is Mr. Smith who is kind and who was, I think, glad that I came. Six-thirty and we were eating in the student dining hall, one room, a prayer, good food served by students in white jackets (they get out of chapel as a reward). After dinner, Egypt (the smoking area) consisting of the side wall of a building, two benches, and an ash can. Mr. Smith called the eight legal smokers the "rebels," the "restless students," but I was with them alone for ten minutes, and had my after-dinner cigarette with them. They were no more restless than I, except that they were obviously dominated by one person, blond, cool, Camels and Weejuns, who talked and they were mesmerized. I thought of people back at Exeter like that, and how they wouldn't last long at Exeter as that — the domination — would never hold. There are people at Exeter like the EHS students, what we call the Southern aristocrats, who sooner or later become New England degenerates like the rest of us and suffer from it, but from their suffering comes their strength. They are prepared, having suffered, to face the world which is not all Southern aristocrats who are willing to listen and be dominated just because I am a cooler Southern aristocrat. But that was what I had seen of the school, and if I had made my judgment then (because I make judgments and it hurts and frustrates when the judgments are too easy — you're never quite as secure with your judgments when they come fast) I would have regretted it. I sat in after dinner on a religion class, and they

— bright, perceptive, slightly racist — were discussing *Soul on Ice*. With my usual immediate candor and rudeness I asked some of them some penetrating questions about blacks, but they came through admirably, and I learned more about them in that hour, of course, than I had in ten minutes of Egypt. I had a new basis for judgment — I should say a comparative basis for judgment.

The next hour with the staff of the newspaper: I preached on the ills of an administration that censors and controls a newspaper, on the beauties of having total control (they were green when I told them about our profit-sharing system) of a newspaper. I knew in my heart, however, that it made no difference: we got about as much done as they did in terms of action. We spoke more violently, but I am convinced that change came about because the faculty at Exeter felt the same way we did and would have changed things anyway, *Exonian*, students, sentiment, all be damned.

The faculty at EHS is stuffy, but I think ready and willing to change some things — the same sort of old versus young faculty. The faculty on the Curriculum Committee talked with me, or I talked to them, for over three hours, telling them the wonders of Exeter: the senior project, the Interns, the freedom, the rules, the course requirements, and the ills of the athletic scholarship system (which I hope doesn't get back to the powers-that-be), along with my standard militant statements about the fund drive (along the lines of my violent editorial last spring). But I told it like it was, and afterward Smith said that at age seventeen he couldn't have come close to having been so articulate and couldn't have handled a group of older men with such proficiency and ease. Naturally my ego was boosted through the ceiling, and was rewarded with a belated beer "despite the fact that Exeter's rules say no alcohol," a privilege which in itself was nothing but indicated an enlarged respect for me on his part which I appreciated. We talked for a while and then I went to bed in the guest house, a large colonial room with all the conveniences except lights in the bathroom (I shaved with my right hand and held a lamp in my left), with the bell tower about four inches from my ear all night.

Except that I slept through breakfast, the next morning was rather uneventful. I was introduced by Mr. Smith in their chapel-auditorium, with some wise reference to my hair (a story about his little boy's reaction to it the night before). They chuckled but, to my regret, that was the only sign of life that I saw for the entire time I was there. There must be a tradition at EHS that when a visitor comes, give him no inkling as to whether or not he's there, much less as to whether or not you are there. I was introduced; no clapping; flawless oration with simplicity and depth; thank you; no sound; I snuck over to my chair on the stage; sat down; not a sound. Mr. Smith asked if there were any questions; there was one about the senior project system; I answered it trembling; they were dismissed, and left without a whisper.

In the depths of whatever I was in, I proceeded to a class, but my stomach was growling so I left and went home for a huge breakfast, and was never sure how I came off until my cousin's fiancé-to-be, a teacher at EHS whom I saw a few times when I was there, called home to my mother and said that in fourth period they were still talking about my speech, that it was superb, and that I had made quite an impression on them.

My mother remembered the story of Abraham Lincoln and

the Gettysburg Address — no one uttered a sound when he
was done. My mother does that, you know; she makes me
feel good. I think of all teen-agers she likes me the best.
That's reassuring in itself, and it's at times like these that I
wonder why.

I gave noonday prayers yesterday, which I was not prepared for, and I think I blew it. In my rush at home that
same morning, desperately looking for something to read,
I grabbed Walt Whitman lying on my desk. I chose my
prayer, two poems with appropriate (i.e., anti-Christian)
passages deleted in the car driving down, which is not easy
when you're driving. I read it to about ten people and
socked the Lord's Prayer to them for compensation, muttered
something like, "Peace be with you, Amen," and stumbled
off out the door through which I had appeared, long haired,
not three minutes before.

I learned today that I have had a nickname since the first
day: Furry Charlie, taken from some saying that man is a
furry animal clinging to the side of a star. Something like
that. And I never knew they were using it until today, the
Day, when Peter Lee told me.
I am tired of writing.

So then, to continue, JCH and I went to Baltimore to see
the campus of Hopkins. My reactions to the campus were
that it was fairly blah, that the students were probably good
people, and that the school itself was probably good, though
I wondered why ten of the eleven classroom buildings were

devoted to things scientific and only one to everything else.

Never mind. The important thing was first that Harper took me, and second that we became close, closer during the ride up and down. Going up was devoted mostly to discussing other people, mostly Washington clergy. (An indirect preparation, I thought, for the conversation we would have on the way down, about JCH and CT.) By the beginning of the drive back, I had decided to give the manuscript (why do I call it that? am I becoming obsessed with the flattery it has received, the compliments I should say because they are sincere) to Harper when we returned. But we discussed it, I pretending that Lee hadn't seen it, he pretending that he didn't know Lee had seen it, all of which I found out this morning when the die had been cast. But we discussed me and him, and him and me, and it was good. I was at my most honest about telling him how to read it (the whole thing before he said anything to me) and he saying that I could trust him, that I did trust him, was true. Frankly, my reservations had gotten over the stage of not wanting him to see my criticism, but were at the stage of his possibly losing respect for me because of my sordid life. But I knew that I had to show it to him, for me, for him, for us most importantly, and after this morning, I am satisfied that I did.

I spoke to Lee when I came in this morning, and he told me that Harper had read it and was touched, moved by it. I was relieved and still more glad that I had shown it to him. The only indication I had that he had seen it was his knowledge of my reaction to the first day, when he told me I ought to wear a tie. This morning about ten he walked up to me and said "How's your tie?" and took it and straightened it

for me. Let me say that if there was ever a moment when I
loved John Harper that was it. Boom. Then the touching
moment when I came into his office and said I was ready to
go and take him somewhere in the car. He said, "Close the
door," and I obeyed and thought whatever it is you think
when someone tells you to close the door. He pulled out
some sheets of paper; I remembered he had told me that he
had written some poems long ago that he never showed to
anyone. He read them, they were good and genuine, and I
could see him in the past and I could see that yes, he does
hurt in the way that everyone should, in the way that I
should. I was too touched to respond, he too nervous to
really let me respond, and we were both, then, absolutely as
human as we could be. He told me some of his reactions to
my paper, that perhaps "asensitive" was the word to describe
him, that all was true but that he had to show me he was
sensitive. It didn't matter because I knew it, and I knew the
moment I decided to let him see it that he was a feeling
person, and that his telling me and showing me that meant
we were friends.

   This morning Peter — why do I call him Peter in this?
I call him Mr. Lee to his face but he is Peter to me — and I
went down to the shore above Fort McNair and walked along
and talked about sexual relationships and relationships in
general, including Harper, including the girls. He called
them faceless and I was offended but I know that maybe they
are in the sense that he means, which is that they, in the
paper and in reality, are only kyros — intense experiences —
and not chronos — time experiences — and that they come
out as the undescribed half of many intense events. That, I

know, is why I am young and he is old(er) and I should say
how I am young and he is old. Youth is intense, oldness is
long and flowing and growing, and I am at that transition,
and he is right. He said what I had been trying to say for a
long time.

Exeter

Two

May 5, 1969

BACK TO WHAT has become home and to what will soon never be again. Back to both what I wanted and (what I didn't realize) not what I was looking for. The urge was to return to the security of close friends, of being back in my own medium, where effort is natural, where new is in people, not in variety of experience. The effort to write this down came with difficulty; my first day back went fast, slipped by easily and obliviously happy. The novelty has trickled off into the moments of mild joy when the last few people find me, and I them, and we shake hands or hug each other to say hello. Already one of the ones I wanted to see, Harris, has made me cold, or I have made myself cold with him. Suddenly our difficulty, our strained times, the ones that I forgot so quickly from a distance, have returned with the small jolt of confirming, reconfirming those things which you had wanted to forget, that were so easy to forget from a distance.

After one day I feel useless, a day of really nothing. I

realized once again my extreme need to be busy and after something — what Peter Scheer calls the accomplishment syndrome, although I am unwilling to be labeled as one who is part of that syndrome. But Peter is good, quiet and pensive, and still the same, obliquely warm and wonderful person that he was four years ago when we first met. Webster, good, fast friend since September, is the same, and I have found no fault in him. I was told that he had grown close to George, but I sense that it is another phase. Not that I don't have them, but he gets them, and then is hostile to me when I question their strength. Our friendship, our love, is renewed, and he is lively. Mel is the one who briefed me on the bus up from Boston, who briefed me on rumors, new ties and loyalties, and he is still good, but kind of the same in a tiring way, not in a reassuring way — more relaxed, even lazy, bearded, and happy. But I am deadly afraid that he will soon snap out of whatever dream he's been in for three years and see himself more clearly.

Exeter, Peter, Web, Mel, George, all have not stopped like a frozen movie shot. They and their different lives have not stopped to wait for my return.

There is a lot more of me than there was, a lot more of Charles Trueheart has been extracted and tempered and returned. I look at school, me, them, with more hateful objectivity, which all seems to be rapidly going down the drain. It is so easy here, so easy to be a shit, to be whatever the hell you want. Despite what every one of these people bitch about, there is freedom here, one hell of a lot of freedom, and it is now that I see it.

The shock of the outside is almost killing. It almost

killed me, but it ended up steeling me for a time, a time
which I am fighting this instant to preserve, rather than
slip into the nontime, stop-time. A Möbius strip: you can
continue to turn it and be fascinated until you stop, until you
realize that the face is the same one all the way around.
Then you set it down and look at other things.

Hesitant to draw too many analogies now, to jump to
too many conclusions at the instant of return and realization, but I am afraid of this moment, of all these moments.
They go so quickly, they run away and you want to hit
yourself for not holding on to them. I want to tell everyone
here to wake up (Peter has) but I should shut up. I will
just *be* my realization. I will be the Jesus Christ, the human,
tangible creation of the spirit that moves me now and forever. I will forget my responsibility to others, draw a
curtain around my newness, around what I have to offer, to
help (I do, I do) and will either weep or snicker as the others
fall deep.

The possibilities which confront me are endless, but they
will be determined by me and only me, and that is what I am
most concerned about, that they do become the products of
me. Of course the answer is you're wedged Charlie, there
will be others who will influence you just like so many people
have before. My answer is yes, but now I have found and
been faithful to my foundations. I have found them, or at
least I know what they feel like, though I have only glimpsed
them.

I feel detached, and I am worried, right now, that detached may become closed. I have written this for no one
but myself.

I would write of even more initial reactions than this but

they have come, surged, and gone, probably as these will. Let me remember through this what I am right now, and the more I change, the more right Jennifer will have been.

May 6, 1969

PART Two of the project: the local church. Bosses: Reverend Lloyd Fonvielle; Reverend William A. Hills. Location: Christ Church, Exeter. Here I am. I saw Fonvielle this morning, and he was a good listener, but also a heavy talker, and the simplest answers I could give, indeed, the beginnings of evolving answers, would be quickly accepted and dropped so that we could get on to whatever he had in mind before he even talked to me. He asked me what questions I had when I went into Part One in Washington, and if they were answers, and what questions I had going into Part Two. I gave him the surfaces of three answers which were quickly taken and thrown aside. But I mentioned a few things that I learned in Washington, sort of accidentally and indirectly, and those were the most important things, about myself, which will remain with me for a long time. I also told him about me in relation to others, things that I cannot explain but only know.

Today I received through the kind words of the principal the word from Amherst, which was no. Finally I approached what is and will be reality. I will be far, new, challenged, and will come out stronger but with a little less love. I will go in weak and alone but very ready, searching in every new face, every new voice, for the past, for some friend who will never quite match ESG.

Today I am reading *Swann's Way* by Proust which is part

of *Remembrance of Things Past.* I am comforted, but I also
see the immense tragedy of living in what was and never
being satisfied by what is.

Today Mel and a few others were talking about their summer. The time they would have, and for them (they couldn't
see it) the rest was set and secure. They could think about
the summer and all the other shit that gets thought about
sooner or later. As he was talking, I jumped from my silence
off the bed, out the door: where are you going? out, and into
the street, away. I found myself somewhere where I wasted
away an hour reading. Reading what? The bound volume of
last year's *Exonian,* with all the stories and by-lines of CT.
The glorious past that was so great. I really couldn't care less
now, but what is tragic, not about then but about now, is that
once it was all so goddamned important to me. I *know* it was.
How can I be so harsh on my own innocence and pride of a
little more than a year ago?

So now for me it is hard, because for every friendship that
becomes stronger now, for every person that I love more, for
each one — and there are many many — the pain will be
greater for me when my time comes. As I told Chuck this
afternoon, even going to Paris with two Exonians will be like
torture, like prolonging the misery of departure.

Why is it that I can love everything about school, the
people, so much and so late in my time here and then have
them all washed down the drain forever when I hardly know
their beauty? I said to Peter this afternoon, hand on his
sprouting Jewish Afro, my little *gemutschtellah,* "I'm going
to miss you, Puck." He said nothing. Then, "We've got to do
a lot together this spring." It will hurt because we will be
trying to cram our life together in a few intense moments.

I KNOW IT WILL BE FUCKING GOOD FOR ME BUT I CAN'T BEAR IT RIGHT NOW. EVERYBODY LET ME BE A SHIT FOR ONE WEEK AS I PREPARE MYSELF FOR THE NEXT PHASE.

Quiet. At Deacons with many people I am quiet. It hurts every time I open my mouth. It is something like love, and the pain, I fear it, will be worse. That itself is selfish, and that is what I mean.

May 7, 1969

A GOOD NIGHT'S sleep and I was able to wake up and say "I'm going to Johns Hopkins" and not flinch.

I went to the Fonvielles' house after lunch to begin my first period of work there, and over coffee we discussed mutual acquaintances. I think I am beginning to like him, he is sensitive about me, and a dedicated clergyman, someone good to work with. Hills came in while we were talking. I have already developed a prejudice toward him which will be hard to shed. He strikes me as someone who is personally incongruous — like he is made up of about seven different people, in personality and appearance, and is busy trying to put himself together. But at least he's doing that and not falling apart, all unglued on the floor. I must learn him soon.

So that has been today. Last night, late, Webster and I had a long talk. I came out of it unmoved, unable to tell him anything, unable to make him see what I was feeling. Our conversation was the same, and rather stagnant. He berated his own capacity to love, the strength of the relationships he has, his own attempts to cut himself off because he feels he is so worthless, and his doubts about the strength of the Bull-Trueheart relationship, so great and intense, in the face of the

Scheer-Trueheart relationship, so long and warm and never-needing-to-be-expressed. He is right, but we have only known each other since September, so what could he expect. To let it die just because he feels defeated is an insult to me and to myself. Whenever I spoke I sounded to myself like I was preaching or counseling him on a detached problem. I was mad at myself for doing it, but I think those are the Termination Blues.

A letter from Jennifer, crushing, true, refreshing, stable:

> The day after I read it [a poem I sent to her a week before I left] one of the poetry week speakers quoted someone as saying that one should be suspicious of people who write poetry because at the time they are writing they are more interested in the words than in you — and that's great because words are stabler. What I want to say is that I don't want our relationship to be anything more or less than it is now. I think we're both on the verge of major change; something soon is going to make us both overflow our presently self-imposed, self-conscious boundaries. At the moment, I'm cold, contained, and unphysical but I don't want to worry about it — except that I don't know if I want to be honest or if it matters. Anyway, I love knowing you, I'm applying to Berkeley, and have fun this weekend.
>
> JENNIFER

So I am helpless, except that even though I could argue with every one of her points and be right, I don't want to, because she too is a teacher for me, and I think one who cares. I have known this about her, about us, for a long time, since the second time I saw her, but I have been hardheaded and have tried to do more. Yet she is right. Perhaps my strongest argument, and I might as well get it off my chest, is Yes, but where would we be if I hadn't been so damn hardheaded in

the first place. Things, people, must always grow, together
if not united. But I too will remain contained and will suc-
cumb to her words and write her and tell her yes ma'am
because naturally I worship the ground she walks on and she
knows it.

May 12, 1969

OH, THE WEEKEND. It must be that I have faith because I
have a lot of hope about possibilities in people. I was
genuinely anxious to see Edie before she came; I suppose I
dreamed about some sort of miraculous change that she
might have undergone. But I was dreaming, and the weekend was hers. It went like the two previous ones — in many
ways less well. It was the same old story, she nervous about
me, me nervous about her, because we are both inhibited
when we are together. And no sex.

It is a frustrating thing to sit in a room talking absolute
fabricated nonsense, smoking away at thousands of cigarettes,
when there are six other couples, either seemingly or actually
grooving on their dates, touching, complimenting, laughing.
It is frustrating not because we wanted to be the same way,
but because we *were* the same way, and because we know
each other so well. Yet we don't express it.

But I have known her too long, and we are approaching a
dead end, when mind love cannot continue unless it is supple-
mented and balanced by the physical. I spoke to Peter, the
Saint, about it Friday night, and he told me to talk about it
with her Saturday. We, she and I, were left alone on a
deserted area near the proverbially birth-death water the
next afternoon, and we talked about it, and shat on ourselves

for two hours. She said she would marry still a virgin, and
I said I would never marry one, and we saw an impasse there
already. So by the time we retired Saturday night, nothing
had happened, and we had both turned sour. I saw that,
right or wrong, the burden lay on her. I exhausted myself;
I think it is the end, and I am sad, for me, and to a great
degree for you, because you gave us so much hope.

Now my sympathy is gone, perhaps because I am selfish.
I must leave her: the winner of the election for president of
her school by a ninety per cent majority; the little girl who
played nude with me in the playpen at age six months; the
girl who kept coincidentally running into me on the tennis
courts when we were thirteen and fourteen; the one who was
to be my childhood sweetheart and then my wife — just like
the Gleasons; the date at the dances; the sender and recipient
of up and down letters; the girl whom I suppose I love
because she represented a potential for me, a potential wife
with whom I could remember back so far and with whom I
could grow from such an early age — a dream that is now
gone, and I think irretrievably so. As young as I am, I am
getting old like everyone else, and the wild years of teenhood
are drawing to a close, nearing the age of seriousness and
hard work and commitment. The scope of possibilities nar-
rows, and I must be worthy of my own suffering.

                              *   *   *

I talked about the priesthood with Fonvielle today, and the
revelation came for both of us that what a clergyman must
decide is in what things he has a stake, and whether the
stake is a religious, working (duty) one or a human one. He
said I was a sensitive young man, and I thanked him. He

has an irritating habit of asking me a penetrating question, and after much inner hassle I wring a sincere answer from my soul, and he just moves on to another subject. I am left with shit dripping from my mouth and no toilet paper, if you get the image.

I felt proud and mad at this meeting tonight, because I came up with the ideas, and I talked the way I did not last time. There was a lot of babble going on while I was serious and concerned, doing what Jennifer (the dream suddenly alone, the remaining, ultimately ephemeral dream that comes all the time) says I shouldn't, and that is be serious. I was mad, I exerted myself and got into the thing, really excited, and the shit was still there.

May 14, 1969

SAINT PETER told me that he was feeling for the first time the Termination Blues. We spent an hour after dinner talking about that. It is often good to have empathy, especially from someone you care about, someone you are deeply committed to. Empathy probably isn't even the word I was searching for — commiseration is more *à propos*. But I had it good with him.

Write a sermon, star in a play: the two things in which I want to excel, to do my utmost — the former for myself, the latter for all the douchebags in the world. The others know me already.

May 15, 1969

I THOUGHT PERHAPS that I was making excuses when I said just let me be a shit for a while, but it seems that I am one.

It's all part of the end. We close ourselves to others, we become cynical and nasty, all subconsciously, because we want to make it easier in the end to say good-bye. I was cynical this afternoon, and Mel told me he was going to leave the room because he had given up baiting a long time ago. I apologized, though I felt like defending myself, and I asked Webster why Mel was getting so mad at me all the time. Webster replied, "Well, you have been pretty much of a schlongus this week." I came into the butt room at five-thirty and Puck and Louie were having a cigarette. We aren't supposed to have out of dormers in our butt room, so when Mel came in and told Louie to put his cigarette out, Louie said, "Let me finish it." Mel said, "No, Lou, I said now"; Louie said, "OK." I sighed, started to say something to Mel, then said, "Never mind," at which point Mel turned on me, said, "Thanks a lot," and stormed out of the room, slamming the door. I felt like shit. Later on I apologized to him, and then he apologized to me, and either neither of us believed it or both of us did. It gets me down.

I was sad that no one felt the nostalgia of the last Deacons meeting, that we all trickled out at the end without knowing it, Chuck and Bishop and Jeffrey and a few others whispering and giggling in the background. I realized and felt my first termination "rush" (as we call it in the drug underworld) when on my way back from Dramat House tonight I suddenly wanted to cry and I did, very briefly, for lost times. I stopped because I think the full force had not hit me, the far-reaching consequences of *leaving these people and this place* just haven't come yet. They begin to approach the climax when you get a feeling for what it will be like, when you then begin to feel the rushes, then more rushes, and I imagine one day boom and there will be tears.

May 16, 1969

I THINK BACK over all of the things I've written and it seems things have been and are going down the drain, degenerating so that life has become much time and very little times, in the old distinctions made by the Greeks. When I sit down to write this, I try to remember something particular during the day to talk about and it isn't really there. So I have to either make up or blow up something that wasn't really important, or write of nothingness.

At Christ Church I found myself bored, not because anyone there was not doing his duty in finding me things to do, but because I didn't feel like doing anything. I came in and talked to Fonvielle for a while. Some woman came in and started to talk about something. I sauntered out and picked up the *New York Times* crossword and drank coffee until noon.

Webster and I became suddenly aware that it would be nice to turn on just once and almost did it late tonight, not five minutes ago until I said no and he said no, and besides it was all academic since there was nothing here anyway. God help us if there had been. Going over to talk to you about my sermon: sherry wafting from your glass, merging with the waft from your mouth, talking with your wife, who knows it will soon be over. I do too. We don't do anything on nights like these but talk and sing old tunes in the butt room, surprising Mr. White when he came up tonight to tuck us in. Yes, that was my hard day.

The last moments together and we must be like this, we must destroy the mellow for the exciting, for the last hash-bash together, for the moments of absurd mindlessness. It's so much easier than keeping our commitment to life, to each other, and to whatever it was back when it was good, when she was good. I often think of Jennifer but she is distant, and also very far away.

I realize that just being CT doesn't mean that people will love you, especially right away. You can be sure of that. Maybe to be sensitive to what others are feeling is not really to be yourself, unless that act, if it exists, is a part of you. Yes, I see it now. It's getting hard to be someone, but it all works out; you know I think that you'll agree, because I must.

May 18, 1969

RELIEF, PERHAPS TEMPORARY, after the climax, the sermon given and the play given up. I am refreshed and new after a hot shower with the make-up and the day's sweat rinsed away — a spiritual shampoo if you will, a religious sudsing.

I was nervous about the sermon until this morning, when reading over the text out loud in one of the church's basement classrooms, I suddenly realized that it was OK. Not as good as the EHS sermon, but now that too didn't matter either, because I was not only trying to do well, and I did want to do that, but worse, I wanted to jerk tears from the old ladies. And I wanted to do well for you. I wanted to impress, and judging from the silence, I guess I did. When your wife told me about Peter crying, I suddenly knew why he was so quiet today. He was crying for *us*. Seeing me up there at the pulpit made him think of us four years ago, how far we had come, how soon it would end. I wish that at this state I too would cry. I think I will cry soon, when the rushes become real and permanent, but saints always cry first.

The play was really nothing: a bit of nervousness, the eagerness to prove to someone (me) that in five days I could do it and also give a good sermon. The performance, besides being fun and amateur, was probably pretty poor. I don't think I can act, and I'm glad.

That is over, and I'm ready for the performance at Abbot Wednesday. There I will be, there's no denying it, out to impress, to win some winsome wench on the spot.

A warm time at your house last night, feeling really at home and for the first time not guilty about taking up your time, feeling that you did want to see me and hoping, knowing, that you would tell me so if you were too busy. Thank you for being honest, and if you have always been honest with me, then thank you for being so kind.

Pleased about the HMCo. letter, but only pleased, because someone, I think it was me, told me not to get hung on it.

The opiated goings-on in the other room have sufficiently distracted me that I may soon have to cut this off. I am still in a state of suspended decision making over the whole question, and I need your opinion, not just your counsel, on the matter. It is so very hard because they are my closest saints — that really was a Freudian slip, I meant to type "closest friends" but I may not be entirely wrong.

Other reflections: dizzy after all that hand-shaking in church, smug for having stepped on the prayer cushion as I walked out at the end, renewed fear for one brief moment when I heard Hills play back about six words of my sermon on tape. It was just as if I was imagining the whole thing and I hadn't really given the sermon yet. It was just like the object, the reality of which is a *déjà vu;* my hearing the playback was what I might have felt had I had a *déjà vu* upon stepping into the pulpit. Strangely enough, when I stepped into it Friday afternoon to practice, I *did* have a *déjà vu* — the very first double-reverse-foreboding-*déjà-actuel-après-vu,* done by none other than me.

Still, the Saint cries in my mind. I want to cry to him but the words don't come into our silence as they should, and that is because there is no reality: the silence is there only symbolically in the midst of mindless voices of zonked and wanting-to-be-zonked people. I wish I were spending the summer with him, but again that would prolong our misery, and Chuck and I will drink much wine, eat much French bread, the blood and the body of JC(H).

May 19, 1969

LIZA A FRIEND, I left your house, Robert Kennedy freshly dead in my mind. When I got to the streetlamp, I stooped and took off my shoes and socks and felt the dust and pebbles bite. Again I thought of the Saint who cried in church, and I tried to cry, but I couldn't. Something had been stolen; I was now steeled for the end. I thought of how I might get you to say good-bye. Two people sat and talked in the darkness on the Peabody triangle, talking maybe of what they were going to leave, not wanting to say good-bye either. Judy Collins hummed continuously in the back of my mind: "Who knows where the time goes? Who knows how my love grows?" Who knows?

Up the stairs I have been up so many times thinking so

many different things, entering my room, finding it was dark, I sat on my chair and thought in silence. Dark and quiet it is easier to think; when nothing stirs, nothing can be seen, not even your own soul. Would I disappoint you? Would I disappoint myself?

Like a signal, a beacon for something to come, the horn sounded, a blaze somewhere across the river: seven, two, seven, two, seven, two, pause, seven, two — maybe a signal for a certain house. The firemen would listen like doctors, symptom seventy-two, according to our records, that's a disease, a fire, where? 14 Union Street. The children would die in the flames, and the tragedy would be complete. The two girls would never miss each other, the first dying for man's progress, the other dying for man's necessity, both dying for the causes that fought, that fight, against each other, dying just as the paint and the sagging couch and the brand-new color television set and the moth-eaten screen door go up in smoke too, in a charred mess while the mother in her smelly nightgown, heavy with tragic sleep, would be screaming in the narrow street, pleading with the fire-doctors to save her children. Her trip to Florida would have to be cancelled, even though it was to help with the birth of the twins of her friend. She would have to forsake another birth for the one she would have to have very soon, when she finished screaming as they screamed so shocked in the Ambassador Hotel last June. When the doctors had all gone away to wait for the next signal, when Mrs. Rathbone had finished reading the newspaper to her deaf husband and telling him how to feel about it, when the night had gone and the mother could sit down and think of her charred children, then maybe she would stop screaming and then maybe Los Angeles would stop screaming too, and then maybe I would. But not until.

Mel came to mind. He has been lonely, downstairs typing while the Saint talked, while Webster read, while George existed, while I lay deep in meditation in the silence and obscurity. Again he was lonely while we danced in the autumn leaves, while we swam in our own wealth of goodness, while we rested in the winter snow tossing out conclusions of ourselves which often missed and sank quietly *whush* into the snow, retrieved only now after the thaw.

Mel was lonely, desperately wanting to cry on someone's shoulder. It could have been mine, but in the leaves my shoulder was with my head, in the clouds, and in the snow my shoulder was holding up my own head, and there was no room, no room at the Inn for the Head of Mel. As my mind scanned Mel, he came into the room and we chatted about the household words we wanted to become, the parents we were already to our roommates, the voices of order and reason and responsibility in contrast to the others. The others led us through moments of shouldn't-but-I-want-to-anyway. Theirs were voices without which we couldn't have lived. Still, the Saint was aloof, alone maybe, because he was neither voice but a voice of his own, ignored in categorization.

Five more minutes in the noisy darkness and I was on my bed, Peter was on my bed, his shoulder on my shoulder, Mel was in the chair three feet away, Webster was in the doorway three feet away, hesitating to come in, and George was in the darkness in the armchair six, seven feet away. Perhaps a symbolic arrangement for me, but I never thought about it as the humming in my mind came to life with the Saint — who *knows* where the time goes, who *knows* how my love grows — and Webster hesitated, and Mel stroked his beard, and George shivered far away. I will still be here when the time does go, the Saint will be here too, Webster will not be sure, Mel will be sure, but not of what, and George will be shivering. The time has been stolen, and it has been stolen by us, and we have sinned, but no more than anyone else.

May 20, 1969

TAP TAP TAP, scratch, scratch, pause, he looks up . . . "Well, Chollie, that's very fine, very fine . . ." scratch scratch tap tap "Tell me, how do you react to it after hearing it on tape?" pause, slide out a Kent, three gone during the sweating painful listening of my sermon, scratch, pscshhhhwww, inhale, "Well . . . I find that forty-eight hours after I said it, first I'm not sure I knew what I was talking about, I'm not sure second that I believed it, and third I think I could argue with myself now that it's over." Pause, sets down pipe, Kent ashes flicked. "Well, that's often the case . . . That reminds me of a wonderful story that someone, I think it was in seminary . . ." and my mind was gone far away, the sweat was frying, my arms were cool and I wanted to be on a beach somewhere.

I bought Chilson Leonard this afternoon and Anne Sexton, *Love Poems.* I read this afternoon and wrote some letters, and went to the Student Council meeting.

Mr. Bedford: "You look like a Mississippi riverboat gambler."

Mr. Ploegstra: "That's not what he looks like to me . . ." and his eyes gleamed, drug allusion, snicker.

Mr. Bedford: "Well, I wasn't going to say that."

Smile, victory over Trueheart. Keep gleaming Ploegstra, I wish I knew you better because then I might hate you.

Bishop was presiding, Trueheart was voting for Feldberg and Connor. Mr. Bedford: "What do you want, one man, two votes, eh?"

May 22, 1969

IT HAS BEEN eleven years since I was last in France, and I remember very little. All I remember is being scared to tears when the horn on the ship blew at Le Havre, and I ran to my father and cried as the ship was mooring. I was three, and I had had my birthday on board — HAPPY BIRTHDAY CHARLES written on the blackboard in the kiddie room — but I can only see back that far because we have a picture of it. And then leaving France, I ran down the hall to my father, again in tears, saying that I would never see her again, my girl friend of age seven. She had been sick all week, and the time we had planned to see each other, lunch at her house, her French apartment, was cancelled, and I cried. The rest of Paris is only a dim feeling of being with certain people, of being scared. When I think hard I can remember things like planting a peach seed in my yard, the seed which would be a tree when I would return many years later, but now I have doubts. I planted the seed in the gravel path. Was I that stupid?

Paris is like yesterday; yesterday is like Paris. I saw you,
I think, in your office. Maybe you were gone. I saw your
wife, I stole your crossword puzzle, I drank your coffee, I
was with Puck, the Saint, Liza was there, your wife, how cold
my calling her that, how presumptuous my calling her Anne.
She said, "Well, the coffee's on and you're here." I protested
mildly but drank the coffee anyway while she talked on the
phone, the long, long cord that seems endless. You can never
go too far with that damn telephone cord.

Mel has some blood, I hesitate to call it Jewish, but it's
there. Huge, fun, swirling water fight this afternoon, the
Saint, Mel the Rabbi, and I, against the Tripping Trio with
water pistols and jars of water. Mel got mad and dropped
his gun and tackled one of them and almost beat the shit out
of him. I think I pulled him back, but why does he do it?
Why a brute show of strength, and what worries me more,
why a show of *anger*? Defensive, curious, hates secrets, likes
to be on top of things, principled — it figures, but is it or is it
not Jewish? Or is it *him*? Could it have happened to me,
could I have been raised the same way, Jew or no Jew?

I saw an old friend from Saigon at Abbot last night, in the
junior butt room (so many hogans, so much pussy, I nearly
went out of my tree). There was sandy-hair, beautiful movie
star. I really wanted to talk to her, wanted to be close, but
she is too too beautiful, so I sat and suavely smoked across
the room, giving her a feeble but debonair eye every once in
a while. When I was in sixth grade, Beatrice (Christ, have
you ever heard a name like that?) was in fifth, and she had a
crush on me. But I only paid attention to JoJo and C.J., my

erstwhile flames of the day, the sixth grade lovelies with surf-
board torsos. But Beatrice has grown herself two beauties:
swaggering up to me last night — "Hoy!" — and we smoked
and chatted until I drifted toward sandy-hair in the middle
of one of Beatrice's groovy monologues. Yes, Beatrice, I do
remember you from the old sunken chest days, and yes, my,
how your hogans have grown. Morgan, one of the fall-term-
upper-year potentials, a tall (you see that was the focus of
our rapid demise, she being five ten or eleven) redhead,
naturally a Foreign Service brat who I first met at a beach
in Maryland at some adult party and there were only two of
us there: she goes to Abbot, and I saw her there last night.
I also saw the girl who rapped at me last year at the same
dance of my first secret infatuation with sandy-hair. While I
infatuated, this dumb bitch cut up the table cloth and gave
me half and I was supposed to cherish it always. Last night
she came up to me in the same butt room and said "Hihows-
thetableclothI'vebeencuttingupsomemoreteehee," to which I
suavely dragged on my haggar and glanced around the room
for escape. And who else did I see? Ben Fitt's winsome
wench who was too shy to remember me from two weekends
ago. And the terrific Anne, longtime friend of Jack Gilpin's,
who is one of the most friendly, warm, sophisticated girls my
age whom I have had the good fortune to run into. Very
beautiful, as it was fated to be, and very tall. Not since prep
year has my height been so meaningful to the state of things.
   At the risk of turning this into a watered down *Portnoy's
Complaint*, I will turn to other matters, like today. I ate
lunch with Mrs. Grey, nice, naive, patient with her kids.
Their lunch, at which I was present, was a fascinating picture
of parental tolerance. No matter how much peanut butter

flew into the air, no matter how much raspberry Kool-Aid
was spilled because of some eight foot straw made of flexible
rubber, no matter what happened, mother had a smile and a
ready hand. I don't think I will ever be a parent. A demon
maybe, but not a parent.

Leaving, who should I see on the street, pedaling a tiny
bicycle, smoking a pipe, all in tweed, but Mr. Fonvielle, who
was thrilled to hear about Boston tomorrow and gave me the
day off.

My afternoon call: the woman was indeed powerful,
indeed more interesting. We talked, she talked, about everything: *The Graduate,* sexual morals ("Mass intercourse at
beach parties, really? Do you really think that's all right?"
and I laid it on thick just to get her goat), politics. (She
makes herself out to be a real political fury — "Fearless Fosdick, they call me in Concord.") A genuinely exciting lady
with a lot of good in her. I liked that visit, was asked back
emphatically to talk to her husband who cannot tolerate long
hair (She: "Frankly, I don't give a damn about hair. But . . .
[here it comes] doesn't it bother you? I mean, I've noticed
that you . . . keep brushing it out of your eyes. And on
Sunday, in the pulpit, you . . . well, like I said, I don't really
give a damn") and to have a meal with them. I may return
to see the woman that some "of these Yankees don't like
because I say what I think," but whom I like and respect very
much.

And then tonight seeing you two sipping beers. Snap:
back to the real business, or art as some noted savant once
put it, of living — the surprisingly mild anticipation of tomorrow at the Publisher's; the good words of poor Bruce
Dobler, who said it was rare and great and fuck you because

he was so much older than I and he had never been published — and I felt the pangs of being a whippersnapper. It
was good to be at the Gleasons', with the Gleasons in a real
moment of relaxation, a moment, maybe even one of those
damned Greek moments, of intense affection.

May 24, 1969

THE NOTE on the wall in the upstairs hall explained when
and how to wake me up; it must have been noticed. But it
was ten of nine before I leaped out of bed and let loose a
string of obscenities. I had to bring her something to look at,
I had hoped to bring something else, some writing in English,
but I'm glad I didn't. I grabbed the carbons of my journal off
the shelf, the first half of Part Two, as it were, and ran,
sleepy, to your house.

I cannot stand beginning a day, especially an important
day like yesterday, first without a shower, second without
breakfast, but I did both. When you wake up, maybe only
waking up an adolescent, there is a deposit of slime on your
face. You can't rub it off, but it feels like you've been basted
with olive oil. That's what I felt like driving down to Boston
— greasy, unshaven, sleepy.

Anne was fresh and vibrant as usual. She asked me what I
thought Mrs. Purves would look like, and I thought for a
while, and said: young, very elegant, probably not beautiful,
Southern blonde. The three cigarettes I had on the way
down did little for my general physical state; released on the
Common, on Newbury Street, I felt encased in grease.

Brooks Brothers first, where I looked at some shirts, almost
bought one, then I remembered that I had better get work

shirts and grungy clothes for France, so I abruptly said, "Thank you very much," and rode down the elevator with a distinguished, elderly operator, undoubtedly with the Brothers since the turn of the century.

I planned my menu on the way up the Common: coffee and English muffins, six English muffins. I wondered at which point I would buy the *Times* and the crossword, at which point I would buy a pack of cigarettes, what kind of cigarettes I would buy in terms of which brand would look the most sophisticated (I thought about Luckies or Camels but I decided my throat and growling stomach could not take them), when I would go and buy Updike's new poetry book, what I would do between now, ten-fifteen, and my appointment at noon. So in a kind of indirect way, I was nervous, but not consciously so. I think by trying to plan every step I was putting HMCo. out of my mind. I managed to walk around and look in the bookstores aimlessly, to try to recognize girls walking around the Common, to try and look like I was first not interested in buying any grass and second not interested in going to bed with an old fag. I sat on a bench and was within five minutes accosted and asked, "Wannabuysomedope?" and I politely, yet courteously and firmly and kindly, declined. I continued to do the crossword, I was having a tough time, when again I saw a very pretty young man walking, swaying, down the path eying me; so I got up in a flurry of newspaper and books and walked away and finished my puzzle in a more public area — like three feet from the newsstand.

Ten of twelve I got up and walked to Houghton Mifflin. I got there quick, like nine of twelve, and quietly passed the entrance and stood on the corner. At three minutes of twelve,

I strode down again to the entrance and walked in to the reception desk.

"May I help you?"

"Yes, I'm here to see Shannon Purves."

"What's the name?"

"Shannon Purves."

"No, *your* name."

"Oh, uh, Charles Trueheart."

You might say I was kind of nervous. I sat down and casually, hands trembling, leafed through a book I was carrying, leafed through a chapter it turned out I had already read. Eight seconds later she walked in and said, "Hi, Charlie."

Elegant, yes, slim, yes, southern, yes, blond, no. Brunette, not beautiful, but really kind face, good figure, glasses, short hair, short dress.

"Why, your hair isn't so long."

"No, it really isn't if you live in Boston."

We rode silently upstairs on the elevator and into her office, small, cramped, but perfect. I felt at ease. I can't remember what we talked about for the first fifteen minutes, but she told me that the letters had been read by three people already, that they were unfortunately all women but that they liked it, that they thought it would be a good idea if I continued to write all summer (to which I said yes), that maybe it would be good if they gave me an option of somewhere between $200 and $450, and — *what?*

Of course, I'd been expecting that they might do something about that, that I might have money, but never that much. Anyway, before we left for lunch at about twelve-forty, I had learned that they were in fact serious about publishing, that one of the women thought that it might be a best seller from what she could tell. (This didn't quite soak into old coolhead until later.) They want to publish it as is. As is, everything, cutting out passages that bog it down. I said I hoped I could keep writing. That's what I was really thinking about, and I am thinking about it now. First I worry that it's too dull, then I worry that it's overdone, and God help me not to think of that lady, that terrific lady, in Boston.

We left for lunch. Walking among people, she was my stylish date. I was bumping into people and she was showing me the way, leading me to the restaurant. I was relaxed now. She asked me questions about the journal, about the people I had mentioned, the ones she knew; we stood in line at the restaurant, continued to talk. I think I was more at ease, or maybe just zonked on ego possibilities. Jesus Christ, every time I thought about it it seemed so unreal that it went away very fast. Lunch: she explained the agreement which I would get for three hundred. I had good wine, good *cannellone*, and I forget the name of the restaurant.

We dropped by a bookstore after lunch, where I bought Updike's *Midpoint and Other Poems*, and went back to the office. I talked with an old woman, I think the big boss of the editorial rooms, and she was, as I was, at a loss for words for conversation. Shannon slyly left us alone for three minutes, and it was like something out of Eugene Ionesco. The idea that I was excited did come through, and she was excited too. She asked if it was an invasion of privacy, and I said, "Mine?" and she said yes, and theirs too, and I said maybe, but that I would talk to all the major characters if necessary to clear things up. She smiled and when Shannon returned, they agreed that indeed my hair was not as long as they had expected. I guess that's the difference between Boston and Washington, among others.

Back in her office we talked about our pot experiences, about the time slowdown and how it was the only constant in every zonk. It was good to see someone thirty years old who had tried, a good sign that people are good, not because of the pot, but because of the attempt to understand, and the willingness to enjoy. Shannon, I called her Mrs. Purves, was encouraging. At one point after we left the restaurant, my mind was so shot with compliments that I said stop and she said OK.

I left HMCo. feeling like sprinting and telling everyone on the Common that I was no ordinary passer-by, that I was me, that I write. I smoked three cigarettes on the way back, one after another. I smiled at everyone I passed, and felt like, like . . . I felt damn good. What would the cover look like? Very simple, just the title and name, no blurb, no shit, just one color, dark, period. God, I was literally going out of my mind. Now I was walking with my arms out like an airplane. I was a hippie. I passed some hippies leaning against the inside of a bridge. I would have been afraid, I would have walked quickly by with my head down to avoid their eyes, but I looked at them, really proud. And if they had offered me a peep right there I would have stopped and taken it right there in front of everyone and said, Read all about it, you're in it, boys, you're in it, girls, because I had a peep with you on May 23, 1969, and you were there to intimidate and now look where you are, now look at fucking where you are.

Racing down Newbury Street, more happy hippies, and me blazer, gray slacks, Weejuns, spotted tie. Me too, boys and girls, I'm one of you despite the way I look. I don't drop acid

because I'm too smart and too scared, but I don't mind
smoking a little pot now and then to keep up with the rest of
the postwar babies, the generation that everyone will remember, that some people may remember because I told
them about it in my forthcoming published book; "a startling,
sometimes shocking, often warm story of a boy and the adult
world around him." $4.95. The Houghton Mifflin Company,
Boston.

Anne and the two ladies were late. I thought about my
mother, and how she would be late too, and how I always
used to read Dagwood when he was supposed to meet
Blondie after work to go shopping, and she was always late,
or was it him. Had Mr. Dithers kept him late to work on a
"report"? They came and I *know* that I was ecstatic, my eyes
could have popped out, but that lasted only until we got into
the car and then it was over.

I told them about it, and the ladies came alive when they
figured out they might be in it. It was more fun to run down
the Common and not tell anyone at all, just know it in your
eyes, just know some truth about yourself and never do anything about it, just to know. If the two ladies hadn't been
there, it might have been different. I might have talked and
expressed the truth, but I couldn't and Anne knew it. She
was good to me as the others babbled.

A ride I will remember, a ride that will be remembered,
and as I entered Exeter, I felt like General Eisenhower
returning to Abilene after World War II, the silent victor.
Anne said that she felt in her stomach the same way she did
when she found out she was going to have Sarah. Perhaps
that is why men are more avid creators than women, why

there are more men poets, authors, painters, musicians, archi-
tects — because they never create anything of themselves.
So this is my baby. They say that in the movies, and I
wonder if they don't mean it the same way: "Butch, you and
Company C take Hamburger Hill — it's your baby." What
foul creation, how foul is anything but a child. For me to be
excited about having a lot of old dead pricks read all about
me is so base compared to one woman — my mother, my
wife, your mother, your wife — having a child which has
grown inside her, and which becomes a creature which in
about half the cases can do nothing but write the same books
for the same dead pricks.

The return to your house: "Trueheart," as I walked away,
and the figure disappeared from the door. It was you and I
wanted to run to you but I walked. Inside, I told you, I knew
you would be pleased, but I was only pleased when I knew
you were, because this book is ours not mine.

I tried not to tell anyone at the play; some of them knew.
I sat downstairs and practiced my lines. Me the author in a
prep school French play; my God, is it possible? I wanted to
go out and give a rip-roaring performance, a really big
shocker of a good job. One of the girls was standing in the
dark, and I asked her where we were in the play. She
answered something that was not what I was looking for and
I said, "No, what *act?*" She said, "Oh," and told me and said
she was sorry, and I walked away and again she said she was
sorry. What was it that was so tragic at that point, what was
it that so unnerved me about that exchange? I had meant no
anger and she thought I was angry. She had apologized and
I had not been able to do anything about it. I thought of

telling her that I was not angry but that was useless, so I said
nothing. I had been arrogant and impatient and unable to
communicate with a peer. My big worry, and there it was,
coming at a moment when I thought I could communicate,
at a time when I had forgotten all my hang-ups for just once.
I am so fucking good with grownups but what about my
peers? What about this book? Will it be only dead pricks
who enjoy it while all my friends say that I'm betraying the
cause, that I'm too nice to the old folks? Will it mean anything to anyone my age? That's far more important. Generation gap be damned.

Between eleven and one we had the biggest shaving cream
and water fight ever — Web, Puck, George, Ben, and me.
The entire network of hallways and the butt room were soaking wet and covered in soap. Our bodies and heads were a
mass of white, me in the clothes that twelve hours before I
had worn to HMCo., now covered. The author at work, the
author at play.

You. I saw you in the Gallery just before I read your letter,
and I almost came back in to touch you.

I remember distinctly seeing you and Sarah walking down
the path on the Common that winter afternoon. You had
on a long overcoat and Sarah had on a blue coat and a little
hat. Alice and I watched you from a distance, a beautiful
couple. In the drizzle you had your head bowed to listen
to her and talk to her in her white stockings.

I am crying Ted. I bumped into your head when I returned. I will never know whether you were putting it down
to me, to greet mine, or whether I just bumped into it. But
I thought about greeting you too, and it felt good to have

Anne's arms around me, because I love her too, but I think
I know, I know I hear what you wrote me, and there is
absolutely nothing I can say. Absolutely nothing. Maybe
we will never kiss or embrace, but we know why, and that is
really all there is.

May 25, 1969

THAT THE SAINT is doing the graduation invocation is fitting;
that I am not hurts. But it is only a final, fatal extension
of the rivalry which began in September 1965, the unspoken
(as is everything else between us) but understood compe-
tition between the two of us. It has been a pointless loving
race between us all this time.

Benjamin and I found ourselves at the church dance last
night, me by invitation, he by invitation from me. We sat
at one of the candle-lit tables and talked through Harris's
golden voice by writing on the table mat, exchanging notes
which amounted to nothing but communication. It was different because each message was thought out, clarified,
pointed, and focused.

Ben asked Zoë to dance just once; I had turned my back
in shyness, reluctant to ask her. Suddenly they were dancing and I was standing over Chuck's shoulder, vicariously
singing along with him, saying to him between verses that
one day I wanted to sing in a band. It must be very lonely
for a singer, because he is only going one way. That is not
like Chuck, and that is why he scorns the idea. But he
loves it, and remembers his Fall Dance date "rubbing her
pelvis against my penis as I sung with my arms around her";

he remembers that, and remembers playing "Back Door
Man" because that is our song, Chuck's and mine, the one
he always plays when I walk into the room. Our song because the first time we got to know each other, last summer
in Washington, zonked at a Doors concert, we heard that
song. It is like a romance, I suppose. So for the final three
songs, we, Ben and I, danced in front of the band, whiling the
time away in a frenzy of jealous movement. We were dancing with no one but ourselves. We were *not*, purposely not,
dancing with Miss Zoë: so beautiful, such eyes, such a smile,
such incredible charm and whizz-bang beautiful exciting
personality. She knew that she had just that at every moment, that she could charm the pants off of anyone she
wanted. One day she will fall for someone, really. Unless
sometime before then she gets kicked, she will not snap to
in time. If I had the nerve, or even the love for Zoë that
I would like to have, I would do it for her, but I cannot
love her because she loves me like she loves everyone, and
I have learned that those little looks mean nothing. I can't
let her fool me anymore.

Back through the rain to Will House with Ben, into the
butt room to watch the end (always makes me cry) of *The
Miracle Worker,* into the triple to listen again and again to
"Jet Plane." Lying on Mel's bed, listening to the whole side,
"Punt the lights," I said, and they were punted. Ben sat
next to the fireplace and dreamed of the girl who first sang
that song for him long ago at Christmastime in the coffee
house, the beautiful folk singer who told Ben she was
singing for him. "Oooooh, Benjie," I always said to him, and

he would answer, "Oooooh, Charlie," when I dreamed and mourned over Alice. Now when I mourn over strange Jennifer, he says the same, but he was quiet last night, curled up, eyes closed. I lay with my head in Mel's pillow and the tears came. Puck was above on the top bunk, not crying. I cried through two sides of Peter, Paul and Mary, then went for a cigarette in the butt room with Drapes. He asked me questions, tears rolling down my cheek as he asked them; questions like, Is it sad to leave, are you going to miss them? Yes, Drapes, I am, you fool; you're so kind, please don't talk to me. I went back into the Lachrymosity Lounge. The Saint, the first to cry, was now crying too, and I went over and put my head on his hand, my head on my hands on his head. His face was turned, there, for two and a half moments of time, our time; we touched, and I left.

We hit the road, Bishop, Harris, Hunter, the Saint and I, off on a tour of old times, on a slide show of times to come, on the drama of now. We sprinted toward the war monument past the Inn, rested, walked on — freedom, outdoor haggars lit — to the cemetery, where I laid some lilacs on someone's gravestone. We walked on past people mowing grave lawns, wondering aloud why the pharaohs had to bury so much shit and so many people in their tombs, why the wives. Puck said that that way a death really meant something. Perhaps true, and I said I wanted to be buried in my own backyard, and yes, I learned that was illegal, and it is like America for something like that to be illegal.

America was very much what this morning was like. It was like something out of Barth. We got to the railroad

tracks and walked down them. We decided to buy a farm
way out in nowhere one summer from now and live and
work. We would have to cut our hair to do it, or we'd never
be hired anywhere. We stopped at a bridge far out of
town, and jumped off because there was a switch there that
someone said might suddenly close and we would get our
legs cut off. We went down to a stream, sat on the lawn
and sang songs all the way back to town, to a drugstore for
a ginger ale. And I split to the Fonvielles' for lunch.

America: Five boys looking for fun, looking to get away
from school, talking of hopping a train and going as far
as it went right then and there, singing, and talking again
about graduation, about driving back. I wanted to take
everyone with me on a long drive back to the South, take
them in my zonk-mobile, which you don't know about; but
much marahoony has been inhaled within that auto's con-
fines, so much that someone once said that all you have to
do is sit in it for five minutes and you're totally zonked.
Yessir, that's true. But maybe you disapprove so I won't
talk about it. Because I disapprove too, but I too, like you,
am a human being who likes to do something naughty every
once in a while.

I thought, before the service, that I would cry all the
way through. I should have, I wanted to, at one point I
even wanted to fake it. I didn't, but I know that the thought
of crying was there, that I would have if I could have. Know
that your sermon said it. Know that you said it when you
mentioned the people who have had nothing, and if they
deny it they are lying, *lying*, you said. It was pointed, and it

may have cut right through a few cynical douchebags, which certainly is a Christian thing to think.

The communion was OK, kind of haphazard and a task rather than a moment, and no one said the body of the blood and I was disappointed. Puck told me later that when he said "The Body of Christ" to the principal, he replied, "Thank you," because he was so flustered, which is wonderful. I like the principal. He hurts inside too.

The best moment of the service was the hymn — Daniel Jesse Wolff (1951–   ), songwriter. The voices were loud, the souls were out front, the glorious brashness of those words socked out for everyone. People whom I had never seen, people who smoked grass, people who did their math every night, people who in their rooms talked about football every night, people who painted, people who cried, people who did absolutely nothing: All were singing and to know that they were singing, to see it, made it a great moment. Bishop laughed and smiled at me across the church because I was beaming. We both nearly fell over backward with joy. *Joy*, Ted, at that service; can you imagine? I felt happy. Isn't that a happy thing to hear? You bet. You know. It was. What can I say but that *I* know where it goes and how it grows, and it isn't the Wizard of Oz.

Tonight, Webster Leland Bull is a hot shit. I love him.

What else but that I didn't see Sarah Gleason all day and that's what was missing. I think you must know that she's a beautiful and charming little girl. Yes, well, thank you, Charlie. Go home and weep and wait.

May 26, 1969

BRUCE DOBLER SAID I had to get over it, Bruce Dobler said he
went through the same thing, that when and if his next book
is published, he may never speak to his parents again. He
said, "You have to make the priorities." But I am too selfish.
I cherish us too much to set that kind of priority. A commitment to writing, to helping old people, to reassuring people
my age, to making money, to making me feel good and brilliant and popular, all of that is meaningless. We have it good.
Why risk it, throw it to the wind, because of my ego? But
then without even saying a word, you are right. I do have
something to share, I must share it, for me. There. I can do
it right and be selfish too.

May 27, 1969

As SCARED AS I was, thank you for talking briefly with me this
morning. Whatever it was you said, whatever it was I heard,
I felt something strong coming through. You have a way of
giving advice, of being right, even of judging, without saying
it, without telling it like it is. You make it sound, feel, like
it's coming from me, like I've figured it out myself. It is a
gift you have, a gift that I receive.

The energy of two days ago is gone. I've gotten lots of
sleep. Maybe an empty day, a day of long stretches with
individuals and longer ones with myself. Sitting on the music
building lawn tonight with Bishop, Harris, and George, I was
apart, silently condemning them for judging, judging them
for condemning, withdrawn, even my eyes flickered around,

my brain flickered around these people. Mel got angry again at me today because I wouldn't support his candidate for council president. Again, again, distance. I must be pulling out.

May 28, 1969

IT WAS TOO nice that I had coffee and English muffins this morning at Harold's Place, after I woke up at eleven-thirty. It was too nice that I read the morning paper there, too nice that it was late enough for the paper to have been the *Times*, too nice that I had my first post-prandial haggar there at the counter, and too too nice that no one in that place knew who I was. That I felt alone was what most appealed to me, that I had gotten out of the dorm without anyone even having seen me, except for the janitor who came in while I was asleep to empty the wastebasket. So I decided over my second cup (with a saucer, no less) that I would not return to the campus today.

Onto the Swazey and out and out of town, onto those roads that take you to the highway, past farmyards and little houses and shade and sun, cars slow and fast and laying patches, dogs, little children who waved. I lay down on the grass and read the picture Exeter Address Book, realizing how few people I can say I know well, how many I have never laid eyes on. Then I slept for a while on the grass until the ants and mosquitoes got to me, then out of town the other way, up to Mrs. Stuckey's and onto the playing fields, up on the highest tier of the stadium to watch Mr. Hall and the Wentworth crew eat and play and talk and laugh as they had their dorm picnic. I watched Mr. Hall and wondered what he would say if and when he saw me through the trees watching, thinking he might come all the way up to me to sit and talk. He finally went behind the stadium, I think maybe to find a place to take a leak. I called down hello and he called back, "Hello, what are you doing here?"

"Observing the goings on."

"Oh."

He walked off and then on his way back he said, for the second time in two days:

"Don't you ever have anything to do?"

"Sure."

"I bet you go off campus every morning and do *nothing*."

"I make the world a little better every day, Mr. Hall."

"Oh, you do."

He said something else, I said what, he sneeze-laughed, and said, "Nothing, never mind."

A letter from JCH today, signed Jesus, thanking me for my letter and maybe saying something about the journal, saying if it ever comes out make sure I come out as warm lovable and kind. I guess I won't have to change anything.

Overwhelmingly, I feel a hunger for something. It is a hunger for activity, for love, for timelessness. What was it that letter said? A good wife, a good meal, and a good trip? I suddenly realized that I have been hungry for the past three days. Suddenly the supply is not meeting the demand, but I haven't made an inventory yet to find out what the nature of the supply is, or why the demand has risen. A cold metaphor for a less than cold feeling. Pow.

May 29, 1969

THE SIRENS ARE going off again tonight, it is drizzling, and tomorrow is Memorial Day, with parade and children and flags. The trains are running, I am alone, and full, and yesterday was an empty day. My journal, believe me, was empty and groping and searching, and even making up for the sake of giving you words. I believe those words, but they were not spinning down into the typewriter when I wrote them. I had to think and remember them.

I have had little tragedy in my life. It is hard for me to understand because I have been through so little. It is so bad that I can't conceive of people dying. I have never been faced with death, I have always managed to evade it. I mean real, physical death. My mother's father died when I was too young to even know it. My father's father died when I was eleven or twelve and I didn't even say anything to my father, no "sorry," until my mother told me to. I was so nervous about facing, I suppose even acknowledging, that someone I loved had died. Three days after it happened I came down and saw my father. He looked down at me, I rushed up to him and hugged him and said the worst thing I could have said, in tears: "Daddy, I'm so sorry about your father." And he answered, "He was your grandfather," and I sobbed, "I know." I never forgave myself for saying that. The other night I was talking to Persis and Sarah and they said that your mother had drowned and your father had died soon after your marriage. That is something I can't conceive of because you don't talk about it, which is natural, but because more importantly, I don't really know about sad things. It is too bad.

I was going to see Mrs. Fiske, walking down that street past Bancroft, when fate did it again. The Trueheart Rationalization Self-Deceit Machine churned into instant operation and there I was, duties and obligations shirked, paddling down the Exeter River in a canoe with Timothy and Chuck. We had food and books and a good time. In four years I had never been on the Exeter River, and had never swum in it. We stopped first at a tree to go swimming. The tree hung, separately and peacefully, over the water, and there was a rope to swing on. We went up on the tree and swung down, skimming the water, bare assed, and played around the river, warm and mungy on the bottom, strangely no current on it. We got out of the water and the bugs darted at us and started a heavy session of biting and stinging that lasted all day. In haste we whipped our clothes back on and left. Dangling on a tree was my watch. That it was an expensive one bothered me little; that it had some sentimental value bothered me a great deal.

And now I wish to go off on a tangent. It occurred to me what bothers me most about losing things. Not that I would take shit from anyone, not that it was a financial loss, but that it was an irretrievable sentimental loss, the kind that I never forget. I received the watch as my birthday present in Hong Kong in October 1963, three months before we came home. My mother and I flew up from Saigon for a week and had a great time. I was the man escorting my mother, the lady, on a trip to Hong Kong. I remember the exact store, location, inside setting where I picked the watch out, our hotel and room number (1134). That is the loss I suffered this afternoon, the loss of all those things.

I have always been worried that I care too much about

that kind of thing. (Saigon — I sold a Dinky Toy to a guy named Jerry something; his father was a spy, he told me in darkest secrecy, a South African spy, I learned later. When I was leaving Saigon, I suddenly remembered that my mother had given me that particular Dinky Toy. I had never liked it much, but I had been touched that she would pick something like that out for me; it was a two-tone green and peach colored 1959 Plymouth sedan, but it made no difference: she had given it to me and I had sold it like a dirty bastard. I could never leave it with this guy Jerry and sleep again, so the very last day we were in Saigon, I got our chauffeur to drive me out to Jerry's house. His mother answered the door; I said Jerry had borrowed a toy of mine and that I had to get it. She said she didn't know if it was OK, but devil that I was [Henry Cabot Lodge once said that I was a real devil inside. He could always see through my polite smiles that I was a cunning little fellow] I convinced her. She let me in his room, I found the car, thanked her, ran to the car in glee, raced back home, and stuffed the car in my suitcase. I have never played with Dinky Toys since Saigon, I had even stopped playing with them when we were leaving, but I could never have left without that car in my hot little hand.) That is why I am sad and disappointed in myself about the damned watch. That's probably why I never throw things away. I have every test and paper I have ever written, including fucking math, since I have been at Exeter.

We spent a great, peaceful afternoon, not talking about ourselves but about sex. As we paddled along, Timothy recounted his previous canoe trip — with a girl — where he took off her shirt, what they had talked about there, how she had felt about taking off her pants at that certain bend.

Chuck and Charlie were rather envious because of course we are mere babies when it comes to that sort of thing. I wonder, were you a virgin when you left Exeter? It really bothers me to think about it, so I'll drop the subject.

For the rest of the evening I felt a hunger like the one last night, a hunger that the cones at Weeks' only helped a little to alleviate. But I know what it is. I am hooked. I realized that I had not talked to you for forty-eight hours.

June 1, 1969

FRIDAY NIGHT I decided not to write anything. I thought that I could capsule the whole weekend, but of course I knew I couldn't. So here I am.

Mel's estate is beautiful, his parents' hospitality large, munificent, and very sincere. "They sensed that you weren't very happy this weekend, Charlie," Mel said to me tonight. Mel, I was happy, I had a great time. I did have a good time, but I could have had a better one; it could have been exciting and not just good; it could have been nostalgic and together but it wasn't. It was just as I expected it would be when I went.

We started doing some "serious drinking." I had wanted to for a long time to prove to myself that I liked it, and I did, but it was different. Chuck and I admitted that we would rather have had a peep that night and walked around the property and talked of mindless things. We sat in the spacious den and drank, I fixing myself and Chuck screwdriver after screwdriver, four each until we were happy and relaxed and we sang.

Chuck was kind of crazy drunk, Web kind of gaga drunk, Mel always sober and laughing a lot, George all inside, Puck not drinking much for fear of getting sick, Ben not drinking much out of nonhabit, and me sufficiently drunk so that Ben and I decided to go for a walk outside the property where I told him a ghost story in the dark. A dog started barking after us so we had to return not by the road where the dog was but through a cow pasture. Mel's parents had sent a search party after us, worrying like good people, and they are, but they worried.

Back to the house, listening to tunes on the radio, smoking a few hundred more cigarettes, and we retired to our respective rooms, all in the guest house, you understand (one of two on this gorgeous property), so we were far away from the parents. Within minutes we were all back, congregating in the room where Ben and I slept. We decided to go up on the roof naked — oh yes, all eight of us standing and dancing around on the roof at one in the morning with no clothes on. Then I read aloud to Ben Chapter One of *Powder Valley Payoff*, starring that scoundrel of scoundrels, Silas Wackett.

June 2, 1969

I WENT TO see Mrs. Colby, who had found and saved the 1934–5 Exeter Address Book with William C. Trueheart, Jr., listed in it, along with her own son, then an upper. She was nice and warm, and we talked about the past — graduations, Dunbar Hall where she used to be. Frank Wilson came in to deliver the *Times* and she asked him in to talk. He didn't know to speak up, so she said yes, yes, I know, how interesting, but she didn't really hear. We talked about the loud

music and how the dean went out: "Do you boys like the
dean, well . . . oh, now aren't you terrible" — that terriffic
smile and *tut-tut* — and repeatedly, "I keep my mouth shut
because you younger people are really wonderful, I don't like
to say anything, the papers just talk about the bad ones but
most of you are good, I know, always going out and doing
things. I must say, I'm jealous, we were such fuddy-duddies."
We heard her neighbor come in and go upstairs to her apartment above, and suddenly *clunk-clunk-clunk* down the steps
and we all rushed out, I thinking the poor old thing had
fallen. All we found was a jar of apple sauce thumping down
each step, the old woman all atwitter and trembling, dropping her purse, saying Glory be. I helped by carrying the
apple sauce up, she still trembling madly and pecking around
for things she had dropped, and goodness gracious and all.

Lunch, cleaning out my room. I found things that I never
remembered having owned, and like the Dinky Toy and the
watch, I couldn't part with any of it, old magazines, old
things I had written, or bought, or mostly been given. I
found a picture Exeter Address Book of my prep year which
I looked over in the butt room with Puck and Chuck. We
laughed. We were wimps — tiny, short haired, dimpled,
innocent little ones with crying mothers and stern yet tender
and proud fathers, lonesome little brothers and inquiring
relatives — arriving in this maze of red brick and people, all
older and scornful. There was no one to love right away, no
one you could admit it to even if you did. You couldn't even
admit it to yourself. Any ideas you might have had along
those lines, of loving a friend or an older person, were quickly
gone by studied exercises in cynicism and one-upmanship.

All-stars, class presidents, snowmen from previous day schools, now thrown into a big ocean with so many others. The president, the lover, the genius was now no longer so.

Someone with a high voice and inordinately large hips and a sunken chest with big nipples (oh but fellas, the doctor said it's not abnormal, only extra tissue which will go away): two years I lived with that, with a little body and a C+ average. Two years of no recognition until finally my name became known: by Charles Trueheart, by Charles Trueheart, soon the first member of the class of 1969 named to the Editorial Board, success. Gleason in the Grill one day: "My God, are you writing the whole *Exonian?*" Pride, all the friends, the right people were there, the obituary for Gillespie discussed in Religion Six. "Trueheart's sure to get the presidency." "No, sorry, but he's an OK guy," "Officious, Harvard type, and besides he lives in Williams House," "Yeah, is he a head?" "I don't think so." Now none of it really matters; it is the people I will miss: the people I was officious to, I was pompous to, will always remember me as such. That's what's regrettable, not any of the other crap.

Yes, I cleaned out my room today, and found all the love letters from Barbara, the pert, hot lass on the beach in South Carolina, the passion, the stories I would be able to tell, the distance that would provide an excuse for never seeing her again, the perfumed, loving letter of missing and crying. It was handsome, wimpy, little me fresh out of my mother's arms into that of a precious little woman.

And then to your office, and Puck came over, and then Eric, and then you, and then Albert, and for the first time I was disappointed in you. It was as if he had stubbed his toe

— "What happened?" "Oh." I wanted to get up and ask everyone to leave and leave the two of you alone to talk. He came to see you; he was in a bad way; he was getting kicked out; and suddenly it wasn't serious to you. Didn't I see things clearly? Had you talked to him before? Did he know what you were feeling? I knew, I hoped, that you were feeling something, but you said nothing. Maybe he didn't know you as well as I. He might not have known what you were feeling, what you were being, he who may leave this place tomorrow, within minutes, or even minutes ago as you read this. Is there nothing you can say to him? Nothing? I will not harp on this, you have never told me when you were disappointed in me, and I have never been disappointed in you until now. I must say it, and I hope you will too, when I am next a shit.

I hear the decision arising before the choice presents itself. Tonight, voices in the other room, proverbially calling me to sin with them, the sin of the pipe. It is time that I sinned, it is right that I should sin tonight. But tonight it is not a sin. Tonight my mind is crystal clear — this is what I know, what I was thinking in the silence between the church and here. Tonight I am thinking clearly. Tonight, because I am alone, everything is clear; challenges merely pose interesting problems in detached human relations. I know who I am right this second. I am *not* trying to explain or excuse anything. It is too sharp and I am the blade. Tonight no one can cut me, so it may be that I want to cut myself open again and let the ants come swarming in. I am going downstairs for a haggar and a think. I will not return to this typewriter

tonight, and I will tell you in the morning whether it is a sin
or not, and I may tell you, you know I will, whether I am a
sinner, a nonsinner, or something else.

June 3, 1969

I HAVE NEVER felt more alone all year than I do now, no more
disgusted, disappointed, and above all unable to speak or do
anything about it.

The Saint (he is still the Saint if indeed saints have been
known to be wrong and cruel): "Feel what you want, but for
Christ's sake, don't be a self-righteous asshole about it."

No, Peter, that wasn't it. I was mad because yes I have to
go to Concord. I want to go to Concord, but I want to do so
much else and I am merely sighing at the reality, ugly or
beautiful, that *is.* You jumped, Peter, on me, and it hurt
badly, not because of what you said, but because *you* said it.

Anne: "Did you sin?"
"Yes."
Anne: "Go on, 'fess up. He's in his office."
And that was all. I went and saw you, and we talked about
important things, but we finally got around to what we both
had been waiting to talk about. That distant silence, mine,
yours, trying to figure what to use to fill it up. We talked in
abstracts, and it was good, it meant a lot to me. I've thought
a lot about it since then, and it's one of those times when I
say that there is too much that says no, too much — enough,
even, to conquer the why not. Is that what the Devil is? Is
his alias called Shit Man, Why Not? I think so. But at least

I won't sin again here. That's a statement and not a promise.
A promise would mean little to either of us at this point.

Timothy said tonight that you just have to decide which of
the many things you are going to do at the last moment.
I guess this is it again, the road not taken. Peter before
chapel said that you've had four years and these last few
days aren't going to mean any more than any three days in
the long run. True, but when you are young and want to do
things, people shouldn't tell you what the reality is, people
should let you be idealistic because in five years you won't
have any idealism left. Youth should be a time when you do
all those things that you will never do otherwise, a time to
have fun and think what you want and even turn on. Reality
or no reality, when I am twenty-three, there will be nothing
but reality. Let me have my turmoil. Don't tell me what is,
tell me what might be, tell me there are so many possibilities,
so much choice and hope, and then let me burn myself. Don't
try to warn me about it. Please.

This afternoon I was in the triple and I picked up a note-
book and opened it and read three pages and realized that
it was Webster's journal. Being a human being of sorts, I was
somewhere between outrageously eager and uncontrollably
hungry to read the entire thing, which I did. Some guilt,
quickly overcome by some obscure rationalization. Most of
what he wrote I knew already. That he no longer felt anything for me I didn't know, and I was disappointed because
after I finished, I was not hurt at all. I understood, I might
even have agreed. He didn't mention my name once except
when he wrote something drunk Saturday night. One page

said: "Who do I *really* respect/admire?" Peter Scheer (Webster refers to Peter as the "Great God Peter"), Eric Forbes, some minister, then "Father." Just those four. I had thought that even if he didn't like me, as a matter of fact, *because* he didn't like me, then it was because he respected me and I scared him. But no.

*   *   *

I, leaning out of the window where he and George were sitting on the porch, talking:
"Hi."
"Hi, come on out."
"No, I don't want to."
"Come on, Trueheart."
"No."
"Don't tell me you're going to write your journal."

*   *   *

I went to bed late last night. It is time to go to bed early tonight. Good night.

June 4, 1969

WE HIT THE road for Concord. Once there, trees, old buildings, no red brick campus, a beautiful chapel all old and wooden, no one around. We turned on the music and figured out the communion and those of us who had to prepare things to read did so. We went to one of the dorms and found Sarah and Nina, our hostesses. They took us to the house with the pool — where Nina lived. So we went swimming, just the boys, in the nude. Nina brought us food and iced tea and we dressed and went back and put on the service.

I was worried at first that it was going too fast, that it was disorganized and sloppy. But when we got to the communion, and then to the songs, and then on the last song after my prayer, "Who Knows Where the Time Goes?" all the girls started singing with us and with the record. I knew then that it had hit the mark, that for the last time we had done it again. Finishing off the wine, passing and throwing more Body and more Blood to all the girls, laughing and singing with the tape as we played it back over and over again.

Then, as people are wont to do, we split up and I went down to the river with some girl, talking, climbing in trees, then back to the campus where we ate dinner on the lawn with about twenty girls. Walking back, I saw Lucy, of some fame in my life.

I guess she had seen me; her head was hanging down. I said, "Hi, Lucy." She looked up and I stuck out my hand and still no words from her. "How have you been, Lucy?" "Oh, much better." What an enigma, shy, beautiful, enigma who doesn't speak but smiles. I took her out on a blind date, disastrous, last October in Boston. The only good part of it had been retreating to the car, the two of us, and talking madly for an hour, then back to the grind of a wild date. I wrote her soon after, one of my typical honest open forthright and scaring letters which was answered promptly in *March* with the usual bullshit prep school letter. But tonight at Concord she was just amazing, still no words, sitting down in that group for dinner, she far away talking to other people,

and I watching her and finding her staring at me and then
she quickly looking away. I am such an easily infatuable
person.

We played Frisbee and went back to the pool at Nina's
house. Wanting to go swimming again, a very strange situation what with the lack of bathing suits and all, social teach-
ings holding us back from going skinny dipping, but guess
who — Bishop — yanks down his trou, penis abobble(liter-
ary allusion to Updike's "The Hermit"), and jumps into the
pool. Temporary anger at him because some of the girls had
really freaked out when they saw that, but soon all of us had
our trou off and we were in the water. The girls removed
their clothing and came in: a great, perfectly unreal time
playing nude in the water with half-nude girls, all beautiful
and laughing. Lucy too, wearing no bra. I was proud of her
and surprised and of course a little desirous, what with a
strange little rip in front of her — shall we say — panties?
But still swirling green eyes and a little smile so mysterious
that being the way I am, it drove me up the wall. I even
decided that I had better wait before I got out of the water,
what with things standing up the way they were.

But that was only a particular time. Most of the afternoon
it was amazing how I wasn't even thinking that way, no
consciousness of hogans, just having a perfectly unreal out-
side-of-anything-I-have-done time. We sat on the lawn
around the pool and played games and threw Frisbees and
sang. I watched Lucy as she deftly removed her wet shirt
from under a sweater, with fleeting glimpses of beautiful
breasts. Like I say, I am easily infatuated. Thinking of
absurd ways to see her again alone, thinking back on our

weekend in Boston, on a myriad of little messages that I got
from her through Sarah, thinking ahead, and watching her
green eyes.

We left and I gave Lucy the last piece of Body that we had
and said thank you good-bye, and she was surprised and said
thank you thank you, and then as an afterthought she said
good-bye. Waving and away. Back, as we have always said,
to middle class values. I really can't tell you about the service
or about anything objectively. My mind always goes hay-
wire with little green-eyed distractions.

I said in the car as we left that I didn't want to say anything meaningful for twenty-four hours and I still feel that
way. I came back to the dorm and immediately hit the old
blue typewriter and rapped away. I will appreciate this a
long time from now, when I can't even remember Lucy
sitting with me that night in October in the middle of the
Harvard football field, neon Cain's potato chips sign flashing
red and blue above, making joints and turning on, and when I
know that today was not real, but a prolonged caress.

June 9, 1969

THE GRADUATION RECEPTION, meeting people, all my friends
and their parents, my teachers, talking with the principal who
was nice as usual: so complimentary you want to believe he
means it, but you wonder if indeed he isn't nice to everybody,
and isn't that somehow indiscriminate and therefore meaningless kindness? I kept seeing you towering above people
you were talking to, trying to catch your eye, then meeting
and talking with more people, having total strangers come

up and start congratulating me on this journal. I wondered
how the hell they ever found out, and what would happen if
everything falls through.

Dinner with the Gleasons: The cocktail hour at your
house was pleasing. My father was charming and I was
proud of him in front of my friends. Then we went out and
were all literally alone — I was in the middle, presenting one
set of parents to another. I think I only presented, then I got
out of the clash. You enjoyed each other, but sitting back,
I began to pick out flaws on both sides, my parents interrupt-
ing and not listening to what you had to say, and you, it's
just like I said, I have left you and I can't remember what it
was that irritated me about you because now, at home in
Washington, I miss you.

But there was an uneasiness in the air and I suddenly felt
oppressed, squeezed in that bench behind everyone. I had to
get out of there, so I went to the john quickly.

This is why I was so depressed Friday night. First, Josh
set me off by being so rude to your children. Yes, he is eight
years old; yes, he is a boy. But that is no excuse for him to
act the way he did, and I was ashamed of him in front of you.
I suppose that it was the same problem with Mama and
Papa. I had expected them all to be so great for *you* and
when they weren't I was ashamed. The problem being not
that they were any less than they are, but just that. They
were just as they always were, perhaps a little nervous, but
that was to be expected. I was nervous too. But they weren't
perfect. Papa was nervous, mistaking my friends, forgetting
their names. I was rude to him when he started making
mistakes, and that too was bad, but I was expecting a lot.

They left because of Josh, and that increased my anger at them and at Josh for managing to ruin everything.

I was very lonely. They all went back to the hotel. I was alone because there were so many people around who weren't. I went to the dance for about ten minutes and everyone was having a great time. My feeling was both that they shouldn't have been having a great time and that I should have but couldn't because I didn't have anyone to invite up to the dance, glad that I didn't, pissed that I didn't. So I went out and walked around the grounds, getting completely soaked in the rain.

I walked the Quad for about half an hour, thinking how symbolic I was, going from the center to the steps of each building in the pouring rain, and thinking about all my teachers, then walking up the steps of the Academy building, remembering when I had first seen SCREW THE BLUE written in paint on the steps, how that had been the big thing for seniors back in those days. It was different now. I composed the official poem of the class of 1969, which ended dramatically with the Academy Building bell tolling eleven, the exact number of stanzas that I had composed and then forgotten.

Down to the Grill for a cigarette. Chuck and Zeke were there with people. They understood, and they were good not to ask me why I looked like shit, or What's the matter? because they didn't know and at that point I didn't know, and they knew that no one did.

The Saint, one of the people I will miss the most, was not dancing as he had been before, loving the music and clapping his hands and laughing. He was like me except that he was crying hard, his eyes were shot. I walked up to him and we leaned against each other for a moment, and then I walked out.

The next morning the sun was shining. The death had come. The rationalization of new life had begun. People were busy and quiet. I went to breakfast in the dining hall, then back to my room to finish packing. My parents arrived about nine-thirty with Joshua and cameras. They went off to breakfast with the Scheers while I used the car to mail some boxes of books at the post office. More pictures afterward. Bucky remembered Papa at the Grill, and I told them to go off and get a good seat.

We assembled on what used to be called Easy Street. Now it has no name. I suppose someone changed it, or decided it was inappropriate. But we were there, all two hundred and sixty of us, in suits, with haircuts, sweaty hands clutching the program, reading and rereading our names on the class roll or the honors lists. The Saint, Bishop, and Harris were sort of mumbling together and looking quietly official. My pangs of jealousy had gone, only the remaining continuous envy that I have had for four years was there. The desire to make a name for myself and to be respected — not by adults, nor loved by little children, but to be respected by my peers — was there. This had never happened. I knew that I was liked, I could tell that, and maybe that's all that matters. Finally it was dying, all the pain that I had gone through when time after time my name failed to appear on class ballots; all the needless pain that I suffer because I am always too eager, because I want to please my parents — my father especially because he did so well — the urge and desire to excel, but not quite ever making college at age sixteen, not quite getting Phi Beta Kappa, not quite taking all the honors. I had the real stuff, the friendships and loves, but I am not the kind of guy you respect more than yourself. I don't think I am bitter, and I certainly wasn't on Saturday — probably just forlorn, probably forlorn for a lot of other reasons besides.

We were told to line up in pairs to march in. The music started and we marched. For the first time, my heart went *pitter pat* — it's gone *boom boom* and *thud thud* before, but this time it actually went proverbially *pitter pat* — as I marched down the two or three ramps to my seat, in front of so many adults and parents with faces staring into the sun, staring at the faces above to see their own son, the one who never wrote them, the one who did so well, the one they always worried about, the one they never really knew after he left, he changed so.

Delicately, Peter stepped to the microphone. I was damn proud of him, enormously happy for him, perhaps more altruistic than I had ever felt, actually glad that he was doing it and that he was my friend. What he said was beautiful. I was praying with my eyes open, staring at my dirty loafers and at Web's left sock peering through a tear in his shoe. How absolutely cool we all were, what terrific human beings all of us, finally climactically realized and then split apart. But Peter was leading us in prayer. He looked archetypal, like something the *New York Times* might have in its section on college commencements: *Radical student Peter Scheer of Poughkeepsie, New York, delivering the . . .* The graceful, curly-headed leader behind everything. We had fought happily for four years to see who would come out best, and every time I said, "You see, you won." Here was his final victory, but then he would say that my success was infinitely greater — and so it still goes on.

Bishop of course was terrific. My mother was fanning herself in the hot sun, staring at him as he spoke extemporaneously. Father looked distinguished and interested and bright. Josh was nowhere to be seen. I learned later that he was bored (I could actually understand that for a boy of eight) and that he was crawling around. Persis and Sarah were sitting on the grass watching and nowhere were you but I had to assume you were there.

The diplomas were handed out for a long time. "Charles Trueheart." The principal: "Your parents have come a long way, let's move out where they can see you." (I was right behind him when they called my name, hidden when he shook my hand and handed me the diploma.) "Thank you, thank you very much."

Me: "I should be thanking you," and he smiled and our hands let go.

I lit up my cigarette, the first in my little clique to get the diploma, the first to have a legal haggar outside on campus. The last name was called, the whole semicircle broke up. I hugged Webster and then Scheer and then Bishop and then Harris and then Feldberg and then we sat back, standing up. Leaning back on the hugeness of it all: people I knew less well walking up and congratulating me, Zoë coming up and kissing Mel. So when she came over to me I was ready. I took full advantage of the situation, grabbed her, she tried for the cheek but my mouth was on her neck for a fleeting, biting instant, and then away, her smile beautiful. My parents got a hug too, and Josh got picked up and everyone was around and around. Peter and I wanted to go to the post office for a last check and as we started over we saw the dean standing alone on the lawn with his wife, watching from a distance, a faint, quiet smile. We said good-bye and thanked him. I think he was pleased that he wasn't hated, maybe pitied at that instant and maybe even loved. Back to Will House where we got in the car, Puck's car, and drove to the Gleasons. We caught both of you (you couldn't escape then), talked for a minute and said we would be back that afternoon.

I took the car and hung your banner on the wall. I designed it and Mama made it. I was afraid she would do it wrong but she did it right.

When I got back to the dorm, my parents were irritated; Mr. Grey's party was over and Father wanted to go and take a swim. For some reason I couldn't leave just then. I blew up and they said OK, sun shining off their foreheads, OK they would go over to your office and take a look. I did nothing but sit and say good-bye and make plans that I would never carry out. Yes, I'll come and see you. Give me a ring. Yes, in August. I'll do it. And all the other things that make parting easier.

At the Fleabag-Sheraton in Portsmouth, I sat while Josh and Daddy swam. Mother offered me whiskey in my Coke but I said no. I could tell she was nervous about asking me, and I was sad then, ready to cry but I didn't. We fought all the way to Boston, about I don't know what. I was proud and ready and eager to fight because they were wrong and I was right, about whatever it was we were fighting about.

❊   ❊   ❊

Maybe you can't either, but I can't describe how I felt walking into your house Sunday morning with Puck, before we drove to Poughkeepsie. I didn't even expect that I would do it, even though I had planned to come up since the night before. Everything was very different. Puck and I strolled in, had a cigarette, and strolled out.

Puck: "We've got to go get gas, we'll be right back."

You: "Right. OK." (Your terrific shy smile.) "See you around." (We walked out the door, down the hall in the dormitory, and Anne came to the door and stuck her head out.)

She: "See ya."

We: "Yeah."

Out of town, gas and cigarettes, all the way to Poughkeepsie, taking turns driving, sleeping, talking about school and Ralph Nader and safety. I worried about having an accident. Once as I was falling asleep I dreamed we hit something and the roof of the car was sliced off. Peter was decapitated but since I was asleep on the reclining shotgun I was OK. Was that my subconscious driving away: kill, kill, kill? I think not, since the last thing I remembered before I went to sleep in the car was that it was not Puck but my father driving. That was the only way I could get to sleep. There's something secure about having your papa driving. It's like the way I had complete trust that you would not kill us all on the road to the restaurant Friday night.

In Poughkeepsie I found my way to the Scheers'. We had dinner and went out and got zonked with some friends of his, had *crêpes suzettes* in his kitchen when we got back, went to bed, and I was off the next day. Driving home I was hoping I would be clear-headed enough to think, but I wasn't, only clear enough to drive.

Dinner with my folks, which consisted of restrained anger, unrestrained anger, and roast beef. I was sad that it had to be this way, but they were being nosy and overreacting to everything I said and did. I was being selfish and unfriendly, so it ended up with a mildly furious discussion about the length of my hair. I said it was not worth talking about and I would get it cut, and my father challenged me and said what *is* worth talking about, and then went on a tirade about my generation not wanting to talk when all they talk about is talking about it.

No matter how much shit they are given, no matter how much shit they should be given, no matter how shitty they are, I like debutante parties. I spent most of last evening with Jack and his friends, first at the Gilpins' where they had a dinner for fifty. I had three gin and tonics before dinner and three at the party itself, but I managed to stay fairly sober most of the evening, enough to see some old friends, be remembered by a student at EHS who couldn't stop telling me how great my speech had been and how thrilled he was to talk to me in person, and enough to get put on the lists for five more debuts this week.

It was fun, no one took it too seriously, which is important. These people I know, the ones who were there, are the society of my generation, and no matter how liberal I am, I still believe in being fashionable and lower classes be damned. I get to have my cake and eat it, too. As it were. I really enjoyed myself. You see, I have to be defensive about the damn thing.

Oh, by the way, I got the option from HMCo. when I got back. Untitled, nonfiction work. That's what they called it. What do you think? It's certainly nonfiction, but at the same time it shouldn't and can't be considered the collected memoirs of that famous whatever, Charles NMI Trueheart. Yes, this is like nothing else. What I should do is write seventy-five novels and *then* publish this. Have a good summer.

Paris

Three

June 12, 1969

SUDDENLY ACROSS the room, under the tent at the Sheraton-Carlton, between the heads of penguins and their mates, dressed in black with a gold necklace, was Jennifer. What a game. I quickly looked away and became involved in a conversation at our table with Anne and Drix, who had come to my house from Virginia before the bash. I was distant from Jennifer, and I saw in a few minutes that she had seen me, so we were both playing the game. By about one I got stiff enough to walk up to her and say hello and she said hello and I said I would come and see her soon, but that I wasn't in any shape to talk to her now. She smiled the smile that ordinarily knocks me down; I almost did fall down. I then poured it all out to Anne, how I was madly in love with her (this was after six gin and tonics), which I am, drunk or sober, and how she hated me, which may or may not be true. Anne said I was acting paranoid, which I was, and pitying myself, which I was. But she is still beautiful.

I saw people I hadn't seen and some of the same ones.

There was a guy from Episcopal who ended up with Jennifer, but who noticed? Not me. Also a couple of ex-Paulies that I know — ex-Paulies in the same sense that I am an ex-Exy — some girls that I really didn't know, and one who tried to seduce me with her flagrantly open cleavage and fat hogans. Being the cool unemotional type that I am, I let her know that she was up a blind alley. Later when Drix and I were in really bad shape we went and asked Lester Lanin for one of his famous blue hats which we got and then became confirmed ridiculous.

Today I had the task of cleaning out all my old shit to be stored, and I ran across boxes of all kinds of things. Remember the story I told you about the Dinky Toy? Well, I found the same one all wrapped up in a box and I still refuse to part with it. I found an unassembled plastic model which my father sent me from Italy when we were in Saigon. I loved it so much I never assembled it, and now I have to do something with it and I still can't part with it. What is that psychologically speaking? Yearning for childhood? Refusal to lose parental figure? Oversentimentality? A fucked-up mentality?

Then I found a box of photographs and letters which my grandmother gave me and which I never looked at before. It was like something out of Marcel Proust, to make a pedantic allusion. Pictures of my father with his former broads, with his college friends, pictures of my mother at Niagara Falls with her hair blowing, one of her leaning up against a tree with her calf showing, *risqué* as it was in those days, all the letters my father sent to his mother during his year at Exeter, and all the letters my mother sent to my father during

the months before they were married. It was like what my
mother said to me when she read Part One of the journal: "I
don't really know you." It was so hard to see my mother writing such passion, my father being such a little boy away from
home for the first time. A newspaper article from the 1935
Exonian which my father wrote, reviewing the spring dance,
a good reporting job, if I may say so.

People are parading through my room to see if they want
to buy the house. The real death, I think, is soon approaching, greater than leaving Exeter. Parents gone, completely
on my own, maybe never to live at home, at "home" again but
only to visit as an adult. You really aren't a man, I suppose,
until you lose your parents one way or another, until you are
really independent, responsible for a family or even for yourself, without someone to call when you're in trouble. That's
the way it is, generation, don't forget it; but as is the case
with a lot of things, you don't know how good they are until
you don't have them.

June 14, 1969

TODAY IS Edward's birthday. He is nine years old. I remember at the end of August 1960, I came back from two months
at camp in the south of France. We were living in London
then, and I got home from the airport, stepped out of the car,
and threw up some Swissair food on the sidewalk. Then we
went upstairs and sat down in the living room. I was eight
years old. I saw my mother signal someone in the hallway, I
turned around, and in trotted a dachshund puppy, about a
foot long, with a green ribbon tied around his neck. I was in
tears. I grabbed him and hugged him and read HAPPY

BIRTHDAY CHARLIE on the ribbon. Now he is in the backyard, three-and-a-half feet long, fat, still great, chewing on a monstrous steak bone and not letting anyone near him.

I got your letter this morning, brought to my bedside by Joshua, and all I can say is thank you for everything once again, and I'll see you soon. Things are different now that I won't see you for a long time. When I was here before, I could always think ahead to getting back and talking, and then when I was there, I could always drop by and say what was on my mind. No matter how much I write, I'll have a lot to tell about events rather than feelings, and maybe we won't get to the heart of the matter. But that will still be OK because we know.

Debutante parties are strange things, people are out of their mediums. One on Rockwood Parkway night before last, and I was there, uninvited but now recognized by the bouncers and list keepers at the door so it was no problem. Oh, Mr. Trueheart, we must have made a mistake on the list. I beamed, shook hands with the deb and her parents, and proceeded to the bar. I found a table and joined some vaguely recognizable people from last night or last year. Hello, yes I really am excited about it; oh, maybe next fall or next winter; oh it's just a little something I was writing this spring; I couldn't be more surprised myself; and so on.

She stood glamorous across the tops of a few heads, not just saying hello or trying to get away with as little as possible, but wanting me to come over. Nonchalant as I am in matters of heart pound, I waved her to wait a minute. I finished listening to what someone had to say, feigning pure absorption with my mind across the room. I excused myself and went to her. Jennifer, more beautiful than ever but somehow less familiar, and that reassured me because she is that way. You never really know what she's thinking, especially about you. Tonight, I was not drunk. Tonight I wanted to talk to her. I was there, suddenly she was away from her little conversation group. What's this I hear about your having a book published? I said why don't we sit down; Trueheart had scored one point. We talked about it, and she kept saying how can you do it, you're always doing things like that, giving speeches. I said that's what makes my life worth living, the little things that make one day better than others. We talked all evening, drinking a little, dancing some, and I felt unsure (for a change) because I thought she was more interested in the book than in me, which ordinarily I would have called an ace up my sleeve, but not with her. She put her head down in her arms, hair flowing all over the place. I wanted to grab it and kiss it but being the way I am, and being at a deb party, I thought it might have been uncouth. I was introduced to her friend from school who is sharing an apartment with her this summer in Georgetown. (Don't think I take too kindly to that, what with all those studs all over the place and me in France; but again I guess that's just me being possessive.) Her friend was beautiful, like some nymph who had just sprung from a forest in Scandinavia. She asked about the book and what it was about. I said it's about Jennifer, and again Jennifer blushed without actually blushing. That incredible look in her eyes. (Why do I go on about these women? One day I'm going to get really screwed because one of them is going to like me and I will marry her in two days and then I'll start seeing my mistakes.)

She told me she was coming out at Christmas, which I said

was great and explained to her why. She said it was terrible and 'hat we should be laughing at the whole thing. I said that we were, but that's because secretly we were having fun no matter how shitty or upper class the whole concept was.

Soon Jennifer said she couldn't see straight. I said that she ought to dance, which she refused to do for fifteen minutes and then finally said OK. We did and then the rock band stopped and the fox trot started. She said let's dance some more, but I had forgotten it from the days of Miss Courtney's Dancing Cotillion. She said she still felt pretty bad, thinking clearly but not being able to see straight. So we danced. Most of the time she was leading me, which was pretty enervating if not ego/sex shattering. It was nice to have her in my arms, slowly and slowly more closely together, but I kept wondering whether she was sick or she wanted to be close to anyone or if she actually liked me. I still don't know, which is typical of her, and as I've said to her time and time again, she keeps me on my toes and she knows it maybe.

Well, so much for my potent sex life.

I shopped yesterday and had my physical at the State Department. I visited my father in his office and talked to him for a while, the first time I had been in his office in a long time. Every time I go anywhere in that building, I want to be in the Foreign Service, and there's nothing I would rather do more, with apologies to the Pope and Houghton Mifflin. My father looked radical in his dark suit and a bright orange-pink pinstripe shirt, feet on his desk and papers all over the place, running the world.

I got my hair cut and you wouldn't recognize me. I haven't brushed my hair out of my eyes for days, Fearless Fosdick would be happy to know.

Casey, my friend, came over and we talked and smoked and called girls and played high school, but not really, because you ought to see the dynamics of our friendship. It looks like pure hate. He never ceases to criticize me, and I suppose I never cease to belittle him, but he is funny and good basically. When I'm in a real fix, his love comes out, but it takes quite a bit. My parents came home earlier than we thought. We were stoned and had to conceal that; they were tight and tried to conceal that. My father played backgammon with stoned Casey.

June 15, 1969

LAST NIGHT I went to Casey's house to help him fix his car. It was like something out of "Leave It to Beaver," five teenagers in a garage puzzling over a wrecked car. Gee whiz, Casey, I sure don't know what to do about the fender. It's all wrecked. Your dad will be mighty sore. But it wasn't. All of us had long hair, liberal parents, and had "smoked marijuana at least once." I doubt if Beaver could claim that. As I went to leave, another situation comedy arose, as I found that one of my tires was flat. A real comedy. So we jacked it up. Gee, Charlie, is your dad ever going to be mad. You'll be grounded for a whole week. After jacking the car up in the wrong place, ruining the thread on the jack, using another guy's jack, putting on our trusty bald spare, literally not a thread on it, I drove home. As soon as Mama and Papa had gone out, I whizzed over to the gas station, had the tire patched, put it back on, and drove home. Papa won't know about it until he tries to sell the car with a fucked-up jack. This morning we woke up early and went to the 9 A.M service at St. John's. JCH preached an excellent sermon on interpersonal responsibility, with not too many dramatic pauses. A fairly good service, traditionally speaking — I mean there was no Simon and Garfunkel or Reaching, but it had a certain antiquity to it.

I went to the clergy room afterward and said hello to PJL. I knocked, the door opened with him behind it, and he was surprised to see me. He put his hand on the back of my head and kind of shook me but there was silence. I looked at my shoes, as I always do when I can't think of anything to say, and he said how have you been, and I said fine, and we talked about getting together this week. It was strange because it was like we really didn't know each other, silent. I remember what you wrote me about silences and this must have been another case. It must be those damn ministers, pretend to be so articulate and then don't say a word in private.

At a quarter of six, Jack and Kenneth Gilpin arrived for the ten o'clock deb party. I was not invited, so Kenneth called the hostess and said I have a house guest, but she said no, I'm sorry. But I took them all anyway. We picked up Jennifer at her driveway and said little on the way down, Jennifer of course striking and stunning, me of course swept completely.

The two men holding lists at the door, to my discontent and ultimate regret, were not the good old two who usually do it. Two new ones:

"Trueheart."

"Let's see . . . with an S?"

"No, T."

"Well, well, Mr. Trueheart, could you stand right here for a minute?"

"Gilpin, John Gilpin."

"Yes, go ahead."

"Jack, could you wait a minute?"

"Sure, Charlie."

Some tall jock comes over and says, "What's your name?"

"Trueheart."

"Trueheart?"

"Charles Trueheart. You don't seem to have me on your list."

"Just a minute." (Jock goes over to a file box and starts leafing through it. I wave the rest of the people on — Jennifer, friend, Kenneth.)

"Uh, you don't have me down?" (He fucks around with the lists.)

"No, I'm sorry. Are you sure you got an invitation?"

"Oh, yes. The red one. But I'm afraid I don't know the . . . the debutante. So she wouldn't recognize me."

"Well, I'm sorry, we just don't have you down. I'm not going to be able to let you in."

"Oh, well surely . . . I can't understand it. Would you like to see my identification?" (This was a panic-stricken move on my part to regain a modicum of self-respect.)

The shithead laughs. "No. I have no doubt that you are . . . who you are." (Reassuring.)

"Well, maybe someone in there could identify me. I know some people there who know I was supposed to be here."

"No, there's nothing I can do."

"Well, could I speak with the debutante's mother?" (Another panic-stricken move which, had it been pursued, would have cost me the ultimate ostracism from Washington society.)

"Look, I know how you feel, but there's nothing I can do. You're not on any lists."

(Sweat.) "I can't understand it." (I guess I had used that line a few too many times.) "I was at lots of these things last week. There must be some mistake."

"No. This isn't a *list* (nosefuckingstucktenmilesintheair) party. I can't let you in."

"Could I speak with someone?"

"Look. I'm her brother and I don't think there's anyone you can speak to. I'm sorry. I know how you feel."

"OK. Thank you."

Why do I always thank people? I gave Jack a few instructions and told him to say good-bye to Jennifer. I drove home in a semirage, but it was laughable. I was only pissed because I wasn't invited in the first place.

But let me tell you what I *am* pissed about — a good example of my mother being a true bitch. As you know, we are showing our house to prospective buyers, who have been parading in and out of here for a week. Naturally, my mother's nerves are on edge, and so are mine. So when I came home twenty minutes ago, sympathy for what had happened, and then I went back to my room. A few minutes later, she came in:

"Uh, what time will . . . Mr. Gilpin . . . be arising?"

(I fly into an immediate knowing rage at her tone of voice.) "As I told you, he'll be up and out of here by nine-thirty."

(Feigns she is hurt.) "Oh, I don't care . . . I just wondered if he'll be up at eleven-thirty when these people come to look at the house . . . *from New York.*"

"Yes, Mother, he will, as I told you."

She looks at me and walks away, mumbling just audibly: "My God, any friend who can't even get you into a party . . ."

"What!?"

"What kind of friend is that, goes off and leaves you at the door?"

"Listen, he stayed with me at the door. His brother called for me. The lady said no. I tried, and I didn't get in. I don't feel badly about it."

". . . stays here all night and doesn't even get you into . . ."

"Look, I told him to stay. There is no problem. Get off it."

"All right."

"*No*. You don't believe me. You say all right but you go on thinking . . ."

"Baby . . ."

"Baby! No baby. You don't believe me."

"Charlie, I do, I just misunderstood. But for God's sweet sake, here he is . . ."

I walked out of the room and slammed the door.

A few minutes ago, she came back into my room and said good night, then went out and closed the door. Then I guess it registered that I was typing. Fear. She came in again.

"I'm sorry I blew up at you. I'm tired."

Closes the door. And that is where I stand, sitting up, waiting for Jack, and hoping that *she* will call. But I doubt it.

Is it sincere when parents say that everything they do is for your own good? When they try to pick out your friends and judge them on whether or not they write thank you notes when they stay here, whether or not their mothers allow them to wear blue jeans on an airplane trip? There are some people I know that I would never bring home because she's

such a bitch that way. Every time I go out with a girl who's
the least bit sexually attractive, it's little miss hotpants.

June 17, 1969

IT HAS GONE past pain, past all the tremors and heartbeats of
comic book love now to a numbness which is constant and
nagging, and I think my soul looks like one of those illustra-
tions for headache pain, with the hammers and springs and
little explosions that keep going on and on, all for a fascina-
tion-enrapturement-enamouredness-thrill of Jennifer, who re-
fuses to believe it. If I could recreate the way she thinks and
speaks, it would be worth a million dollars in itself, but it is
much more because I can't, just a lot of expression always
bubbling and changing — facial expression, eyes, mouth
expression.

"This dress would look sexy on anyone but me."

"You don't believe that."

"Yes I do. How do you know I don't?"

"I don't. That's just it, I don't know anything and I'm
always guessing, always."

"No, Charlie, I'm a fake. You don't see it, but you really
see right through me. You do."

"No I don't. I don't at all. The only thing I can see is that
all you do is shit on yourself."

"Don't insult me."

"I'm not. It's true."

Pause. "Let's dance."

Our conversations are either contrived kindnesses, or little
snatches that leave us both silent and bewildered. At least

I end up that way. She doesn't like to talk profundities and I do, and we end up doing it and not doing it. Silence as we were leaving, out the door of the Sulgrave Club:
  "You're incredible."
  "No, I'm not."
  Silence.
  "You're usually happy, aren't you?"
  "No."
  "What do you mean, haven't you always been lucky?"
  "Publishing a damn book is not that big a thing to me. There are more important things, and I don't have them, and that's why —"
  "Let's run to the car."
  "Yes. Let's."
  We do.

I can't leave this subject until I tell you that I have picked someone who is beautiful for everyone. There were at least ten people last night who walked up to her and it seemed as if they had already had intimate relations with her. That didn't bother me as it would have or should have. I was actually proud for her because she does shit on herself too much. What I wanted to tell her — or what I thought I wanted to tell her but didn't have the guts to tell her because I wasn't that sure — was that most of those people either liked her casually or were dying to go to bed with her. But my telling her that would have done no good because she knows what I feel and does her best to keep me at a distance along with everyone else. Last night she began to feel sorry for me and started making conversation. "Will you dance with me?" Which of course gave me two alternatives: I

could be overjoyed that she showed compassion, or be furious
that she was pitying me. Anyway, everyone was crowded
around her and poor little pitiable-to-be-seen me was smug
and cold talking to people who grated against me, people
dumb and full of themselves.

Things take priority over things sometimes. Well, Charlie,
that sure is a meaningful statement. What I mean is that the
rest of the things that have happened seem to drift into
nothing when I sit down to write.

Suffice it to say (Don't you hate that expression?) that I
have been doing a lot of rooting and sifting both of thoughts
and junk that are in boxes. It takes hours because I find
diaries and notebooks and old schoolbooks and I read everything from cover to cover and end up throwing nothing away,
— to my parents' chagrin.

I found a box of love letters from sixth and seventh grades.
C.J. was her name, and she wrote me passionately and
dominated me and I fell right into it and did "all that jazz in
the movies." I found a diary I kept in eighth grade with my
passion for a girl about three grades ahead of me who thought
I was cute and wanted me to hold her hand on the bus. I
thought secretly that she might actually be in love with me.
The things I wrote, my God, I haven't changed a bit, always
swept off my feet by anyone who likes me. That's not
entirely bad, but one day it may hurt, and maybe one day
I'll be surprised to find that everything is real and not
fantasy. Then youth will be over and I'll get down to the
nitty-gritty.

I found in an old box which contained various little papers
about fantasies, a little card which read "God help me to
succeed in Exeter, in college, and in life. Charles Trueheart

12/4/64." That was even before I had been accepted at
Exeter, before anything at all. I was honest then in thinking
that success meant everything, and I suppose in many ways
I feel the same way. But my conception of success has
changed and love is a big part of it. It will be too late if
Jennifer ever reads this, but at least she will know that I
knew. She knows it now.

I have packing to do; Charles Theodore Harris arrives
tomorrow morning; we leave tomorrow evening; I will call
you; and I am taking this monstrously heavy typewriter with
me to Europe. The roving reporter. Thank you for your good
letter, and my love to the little lady and the little ladies.

June 21, 1969

OUR MOVABLE FEAST has begun slowly and silently. The
window across the blue typewriter is open and close to a
noisy, narrow street. Last night people shouted and talked
in the street, cars roared quickly by, young people walked
under the window talking a strange, familiar language.

It is hard to imagine that at this time yesterday I was over
the Atlantic. We have done so much it seems we have been
here a long time, and yet we know so little it seems we
haven't at all. All through yesterday, we arrived at Orly at
noon (7 A.M. to us), Chuck kept saying that the whole plane
ride was unreal, none of it had ever happened.

To make a long story short and uninteresting, we were the
very last plane, so far as I knew, to leave New York, and there
may or may not be a strike of some kind going on right now
in New York. I slept most of the way, and watched the movie
Changes which I had heard so much about and which was

so simplistic and actually quite shitty. We had champagne
to celebrate on the plane, and I had a gin and tonic afterward
and maybe that's why I slept so soundly. I woke up at two
our time and it was dawn. Disgusted, I went back to sleep
until six our time, eleven theirs, and we landed.

Chuck dropped a little package of hashish right in front of
the customs desk, which he retrieved somewhat feverishly
when he realized what had happened. We took a cab to our
hotel, talking to the driver who explained a whole *mélange* of
trivia to us and showed off and told us where to get girls and
how to swear. I think he took us for quite a bit more than
was his due. We are more naive than we thought.

We are living until the twenty-third here at the Hôtel
Racine on the rue de Racine. In the entrance hall there is a
bust of Racine himself, and the people at the desk are kind
and incomprehensible. We have a bidet and a sink and a
douche, an armoire, a desk, two windows, and two narrow
double beds. We took a nap yesterday afternoon after walking around and having a *demi* at a café. Chuck fell on one
bed and I on the other and we figure that Al is a little
squeamish about the idea since he slept yesterday in the
chair. So last night Chuck and I slept in the same bed and
Al was alone.

We have been silent together. I think we are all tired, and
all kind of stunned that we are really here. Walking around
yesterday we didn't say anything, just amazed by the whole
place. The French are nice, but we wish they didn't have to
know we're Americans; we spend our time baiting the tourists
and pointing out who is American, looking at the French to
see how we should dress. I think considering everything,
we fail.

Personally, I have started to fancy myself as Ernest Hemingway. I looked at myself in the mirror at a restaurant last night and was sure that my mustache and I were much like Ernest himself. All of this to Chuck and Al's delight. "To have lived in Paris as a young man . . ." I went out before breakfast this morning and bought myself a *Figaro* and sat and ate my *petit déjeuner* reading the damn thing. I long for the *New York Times*, orange juice, and decent coffee, but don't tell anyone.

Nothing should be sifted out of my life, no matter how unimportant. Because it is all there. I thought a lot about you on the plane, and how I would really miss you, the office in Phillips Church, going over for coffee in the mornings with Anne in her nightgown and Liza in a terrible mood, Sarah smiling your smile, Persis smiling Anne's, Liza with her own when she does smile. People smoked your True Blues every day and you didn't mind, or didn't say so if you did. Those are the things I remember, and I will remember, the little siftable things that shouldn't and won't be sifted.

June 22, 1969

THE FIRST FULL DAY in any strange city must be a long one. Yesterday seemed interminable and full of worries **and** hassles. We didn't accomplish much but we did a lot of walking and sleeping and drinking. It seems whenever we stop to have a beer or a glass of wine we end up back here at the room, sound asleep.

Last night, we went out to dinner at a cheap place recommended by Fielding's, and then to a café where we sat and watched the people walk by. We are trying to get into this city, and we thought this would be the best way. It was fun, and still we didn't talk much to one another, and still Chuck and I are horny as hell — there are lots of girls and most of them walk around with unsaddled hogans, which sends us into all kinds of laughter and existential *angst*.

On the way back to the room, crowds of people were at cafés and around street entertainers. Three shaggy Americans were playing their guitars on the side of the street. "Hey Jude" sent us back and we watched silently, three thousand miles away from the place, thinking very hard and knowing no one knew about it. A juggler or two, a social protester, and lots of girls in little groups of two or three just waiting to be nabbed by three young strangers from across the sea, who have no confidence and only two beds, our daily rationalization.

This morning I got up alone and took the Métro to the avenue Georges V, where I bought a newspaper and went down to the Seine to read it. Since I was proverbially by the water I did a lot of thinking and a lot of grooving on the fact of my own existence. I was right there where I had been long ago, Ernest Hemingway thinking like Marcel Proust and hoping to write like John Barth but just sitting there blowing haggars at the Eiffel Tower.

It was time to go have a mindfuck so I went back up the avenue to the American cathedral. During the service I had my eyes fixed on several pairs of American hogans, but my fantasies came to nothing. I went to the coffee hour and walked up to the woman who was pinning little tin crosses on all the visitors. I finally got to her after standing in line and

she put one on me and I said, "I was bapti — " and she gave
me this disgusting cat-eating-shit smile and sort of passed me
on. I couldn't have been more furious. I was literally shaking
with rage at this old bittie as I drank another cup of absolutely shitless coffee. After calming down and perusing a
few more hogans, I went back to the church to find the
rector. He was baptizing a baby on the very same spot at
which on May 19, 1957, he had baptized me. So I sat and
watched and experienced a few flashbacks. When he was
done I talked with him awhile about my baptism. I was
baptized with an old man with a white beard, I think he was
ninety-nine then, and the rector said he was still alive. He
remembered my parents, was courteous and nothing else.
He said give my best, come again, and I almost told him that
the cross pinner was a screaming bitch but I decided not to
considering the circumstances and all.

July 8, 1969

25 vi 69

DEAR TED:

I am in Brussels now, it is late afternoon of my third day
here, and we are leaving tomorrow morning, hitchhiking to
Amsterdam. Chris is here with us now, arriving in our precon-
ditioned fold just before closing time.

I have spent a little time today trying to rationalize my not
writing you, my stopping for ten days to have a vacation, and I
found many rationalizations not even worth mentioning — you
have heard them before and whether they justify, don't justify,
or even need to be justified is of no consequence.

Only know that if they are important, I won't forget them and they will come up sometime when I am writing regularly again. That isn't often true, we know that we forget most everything, but after all I lived sixteen years of my life without you and got along. You could still know me and love me.

CT

28 vi 69

DEAR TED:

I am alone, riding in a taxi to the airport, and very tired. I am scared of my loneliness and my innocence. Perhaps for the first time I realize that I am maybe too young to be traveling in strange cities — maybe intolerant, and discompassionate when I am not welcomed by everyone, when I am not in the midst of love and the very understanding which I don't even possess.

I fear to disappoint my parents. I keep saying to myself that it's good for me — it will be if it doesn't make me cynical.

I am now in Paris. I was in Amsterdam last night finally after a day of hitchhiking. I sent you a card. But I was here to find an apartment. I haven't, I won't, our money is gone. Even finding Mrs. Henry Cabot Lodge and talking with her for a while was nothing but a thrill. I can't even phone my godparents, I have no sense of confidence. I could blame it on my parents for bringing me up too well to ask for a bed on short notice.

So now exhausted, I leave, and I wish I had anyone to hug, a shoulder I could cry on for a long time so that they too might understand.

CT

The view across the Underwood-Olivetti is of wood. I am in a corner of the apartment-studio where I now live, tucked with my light, coffee, typewriter and mind behind a pottery wheel and a huge black kiln. This is my home now, always, my Happy Lot. Three days after your letter I am still moved.

I am moved but I can only say Thank You. I read your letter to Chuck Saturday night, the night we arrived in Paris from London, and afterward I turned to him, ready to say something, and he had tears in his eyes. A long beautiful silence full of "Hey Jude" and Second Period Coffee and Waiting and You.

I am back. It feels good. I can almost touch you through these familiar keys. It is still tough to be back, like when you go back home or back to school, but you always get used to it and love it. So much to tell you. But I must Rev myself up for communication, so I won't try to tell you everything, but I will slip it in as I go along. COMPOSE YOURSELF in block letters on my typewriter. I will, but it is hard.

We are living together, the Butcher, the Baker, the Candlestick Maker, and the Indian Chief — Chuck, Al, Me, and Chris, who comes and goes. We do not get along, Chris and I, but it is worse because it's under our skins, we don't let it out. It's subtle irritation on my part and I don't know what for him. Chuck is the intermediary, and Al is the rational bystander full of answers that cover half the story — so correct but so half-encompassing.

We began the job — mindless card-punching and filing — yesterday. It will probably amount to little in this journal except maybe my tiredness or my advances on the various comely secretaries, or other fantasies of adolescence.

My address — proud and independent and adult to give it, my own home with people and beauty — is Studio D, 55 rue du Cherche-Midi, Paris VI, France. I wish I could re-

spond more fully to your letter. I can do nothing but appreciate every word, and maybe glimpse various moments of our
life.

July 9, 1969

WE ARE ALREADY developing a routine here in Studio D. We
rise at seven, fix breakfast, wash dishes, ride for forty-five
minutes on the Métro to be at work at quarter to nine, work
until five-fifteen, come back, sit and drink wine and eat bread
and cheese and talk, except me who will go back to my corner
and type until dinnertime, eat dinner around eight by candle-
light with whomever happens to be here (candles because
the lighting is poor, and because we have the candles and lots
of places to hang them and put them, high on walls and in
corners) then talk over coffee, write letters, and retire.

The job is exactly what we (I) expected: all shit work.
Chuck the Butcher and I are learning to take over the section
that processes orders and Al the Baker is taking over the filing
section. We were surprised to learn that soon we would
have some responsibility, but as they say, in late July and
August there isn't *beaucoup de travail.* We pull cards, run
little punching machines, file, order, process, and other
details which are boring and boring to explain. We speak
French and there are comely and uncomely secretaries who
like us and we like them and we laugh and don't really understand what we're saying. One man told us that we already
know how to speak French, but that this summer we will
learn how to chat. Again, I hope so.

The personalities there are not yet surfacing, it being
harder for them to do so in another language, which was a

nice way of phrasing that hurried thought, but they will. We
eat lunch in a little cafeteria for about eighty cents, which
is dirt cheap, and smoke a lot of rotten haggars all the time
as we work. Everyone is kind to us and we are silent except
when spoken to. *Vous ne bavardez pas?* "You don't shoot
the bull, do you?" No, we answer, because we can't in
French and it would be rude in English.

What else can be said? The dynamics of our group have
already become established in two weeks. Good dynamics,
bad dynamics sometimes between me and Chris, because as
Chuck and I decided, he is a sensualist and I am a sensitivist,
and we do not mesh easily or even understand each other.
I cringe and he sighs and it is a proverbially bad scene.

I feel strange about this because I am thinking a lot and
not really wanting to tell you; at times I do but there are so
few moments when I get the chance to sit down and write.
I am feeling a lot about the people I am with and then am
not able to say it. It is perhaps because we are working
together and things happen and little needs to be said about
it. I don't know. Then I worry about the damn publication
and what happens if this turns to shit. Or even if it doesn't,
am I really telling all? I guess I miss being able to phone or
rush over in the middle of the day or night. I miss a lot of
things, like hot showers. (Ours lasts about ninety seconds
then turns cold, so we spread them well apart, turn on the
water for thirty seconds, soap up, then rinse for forty seconds,
then it starts getting cool. I feel like a pile of grease.) With
Chris here we have to share beds. Sometimes I want to cry
for mother.

They love me. They are being quiet while I write, reading
and writing letters nearby, glancing up to see how I'm doing

and smiling. They may still be smiling at me as I dump shit
on them back here one day, but they'll never know, never
really, what I said.

DEEP ONE NIGHT, under the influence of marijuana, Webster
Bull and I concluded that the Johanna that Dylan speaks of
— one's first love — is the one set as a personal criterion
against all others. Perhaps because of the smooth course of
your own true love you never met anyone but Johanna. I
don't know. But I have loved a lot, and I have thought I
loved a lot. She, Johanna, for me, is Nancy, whom I have
not laid eyes on for over two years. I thought of her again
tonight listening to that song. Visions and senses of her
remain, now, perhaps forever. It doesn't matter whether or
not she feels the same or thinks about me at all. I suspect
she does because I knew her well at first and then as time
progressed, not at all. I saw her briefly last Christmas on
Chevy Chase Circle and she was as ever, just as ever, and
she was with a tall, dark proverbial. It didn't bother me,
because she is gone except in my soul.

I thought tonight about the others. Edie; the one you
know from the three dances, spring, fall, spring; shirts and
legs and dresses and smile, our frustrations and one of the last
times I was with her, kneeling with her on a bed in a friend's
basement room, in front of a black light, having fun. She
was purple then, because of the light, and her panties were
purple by nature — she showed them to me. Not panties
really, I must be imagining things; it was those culotte things

which are meant to be seen. It was at that point that I felt very much attracted to her and then that I almost went against my nature and maybe hers (but who knows, not even she) and leapt on her, but I didn't. I loved her then, and a few other swirling moments, and maybe deeply all along. We never expressed it and we drove off the road into a rut.

Of course Jennifer and *her* smile. Last night, alone, I danced with her on the rug to the tune of "Revolution Number One" — slow, with and against the pattern of the rug which swirled too because I was zonked. Jennifer will be my end and is very much my life. Because I am far away I can hope. I could say that I love Jennifer. I do here in Paris, but what does it mean or matter when she is the way she is? Here in Paris miles away, she does I don't know what.

Barbara is of a certain pre-Johanna summer, full of youth and sexual knowledge at the beach. She showed me for the first time in my life, before or since, what it is like to be craved immediately for one's mere maleness. Swept off my feet, of course, but it was short. I wrote a complete record of my four days with her as we drove home from the beach. I still have it and I'll show it to you one day. That was when my father told me that he had been in love too, and that it would go away. I was sure it wouldn't, and I loved him for saying that, and hated him for it. I cried and sulked and wrote because of Barbara and Father.

My first year at Exeter I went with a girl named Carol, blonde and schizophrenic — she said so — and she told me that I was like an older brother to her. I hated her for saying it. We could be apart, she and I, in New Hampshire and Washington and write to each other and most of all tell our

friends about "her" or "him" and get away with it and then
not really have too good a time together. But we thought we
loved then.

The day before I left for France I went to Jennifer's house
for a tearless good-bye. She gave me a book of Ernest
Hemingway's poems, from which I will quote because she
said it was especially for me once. It was one of those poems,
directed for you, that makes you laugh and cry, hate and
love, because it is right but cruel, perceptive but mean.

I looked at Jennifer's yearbook. The class of 1969 included
Carol, Jennifer, Nancy, and a wonderful girl named Mary
Sherman, who led the girls when I led the boys in London,
age nine. On the playground we fought and shouted at each
other and when no one was watching we talked, and I hadn't
seen or heard of her since 1960 when I saw her name and
picture in the yearbook. She was one of the first crushes I
had — right there with the rest of the line-up.

So last Christmas, at my house on Tilden Street, Webster
Bull and I talked about it, and he had a first Johanna named
Lisa. We had what is and was known as a mindfuck, because
we discovered what Dylan really meant by the line "Little
boy blue, taking things so seriously." That's me, and Bob
told it like it was.

End of love life. It has been good. Maybe you didn't want
to hear it, but there it is.

Grunts have come up a lot in today's, and I don't want you
to worry. I know you won't, but I worry that you might, and
I want you to know that I think I know what I am doing.
It's been said before and people have gone insane, yes. And
I am no different. However, I *am* taking a risk, I know it,
and I am not taking as much of a risk as many others. Any

of this can be easily condemned, even by me in moments of self-righteousness. Chuck said that being young is not knowing whether the way you feel is adolescence or life.

Jennifer's poem for me, through Ernest, is called "Ultimately":

> He tried to spit out the truth;
> Dry-mouthed at first,
> He drooled and slobbered in the end;
> Truth dribbling his chin.

July 11, 1969

DINNER HERE and Eiffel Tower at dark. Frightening and beautiful, incredible to imagine anything about it. Like that it was built in 1898 for a world exposition and was due to be torn down afterward — built as art rather than function, and now it is both and very old and more graceful than a lot of modern steel structures. I'm sure poets have written more beautiful things than I about the Eiffel Tower, so I shan't continue. I was alone standing on the highest part, and I imagined myself addressing the world from the spot, crowds like German citizens in the thirties in the streets below hailing their new leader. I even whispered a speech to them about the new life we would begin together.

July 12, 1969

A SHADED BOULEVARD runs along one end of the Bois de Boulogne in Paris, near the Pont de Neuilly. I still don't know what it is called, but there is a small street which runs off of it near the avenue Madrid, the rue des Graviers, and there is a house at the corner, number thirty-one. When I used to live in that house, with its graveled paths and dumbwaiter, I would play alone in the Bois, with fantasies which have been lost but replaced, by newer, probably even more fantastic ones. Today, in the haziness of a Saturday afternoon, I returned to the corner and to the Bois with Chuck, and a lot returned — real things and dreamy things. When I saw the ticket taker at the Jardin d'Acclimatation, the amusement park and zoo, I thought he might remember me, but he didn't, and I had to smile. He still had his mustache, but it was white now, his face had more wrinkles, and he was shorter. I was taller, and now I had a mustache too.

The swans and the baboons were beautiful. We admired them silently and saw the baboons fight and shout at each other like little children, like humans. I saw the little children watching and delighting. It was good to see those children, to see how we were and maybe how we wished we could be. Vicariously I wanted one of my own there with me so that he or she could delight in everything I couldn't. I thought of Joshua, that he would be gone from me very soon. I wrote him a postcard with a smiling baboon on it which I hope he likes. Maybe he will be defensive about it. And he will not be to blame, only me and his peers who have told him not to like it, something to understand but not necessarily to like. I wanted my own children there, not because it was the best thing but because it was a shade more realistic than returning to childhood myself. If I could have had Persis and Sarah and Liza there with me it would also have been nice. It is nice to have children, isn't it? I know it is. Inescapably that brought on the fact that I wished I had a woman there with me too, but that is unrealistic and it is the why that I can't figure out.

Perhaps a lot of your childhood is ruined by older and more sophisticated peers. Perhaps without them, though, you would never learn to grow. You are always growing and learning and never stopping to enjoy, and that is tragic.

I had a girl friend when I was about seven, and one day I asked her to come with me and my mother to go to that park, the Jardin. In the Jardin there is a little boat which you can take down a little man-made stream, through the woods and through a tunnel and then you have your picture taken at the end to be picked up later. The picture is of you smiling on your little boat after your trip. So we set off, girl, mother, me, and Guillaume, our first dachshund, who was brown. I was anxious about the picture because I wanted it to be good so that I could show it to my friend. It was taken, it came out, and girl came out decently after all. Mother, Charlie, Guillaume, smiling (all my dogs smile distinctly), and girl sort of shyly grinning.

Adam lived down the street from me. He was a year older than I. I took him the picture and he asked to keep it. I said OK, and the next time I came over he said he had something to show me. It was the picture, only he had taken scissors to it and only Guillaume remained, because the girl "was ugly." I cried because I knew he was wrong and a shit to have done it, but he was older and wiser and I couldn't do anything but agree. I said yeah or some other lie. So we laughed, but I cried in my room later, and thought of all the ghosts coming through the mirrors. I had mirrors covering one whole wall of my room on the top floor, and they often kept me up all night.

I used to bite Guillaume's ears driving to school in the mornings. My mother was at the wheel and she couldn't watch me. Guillaume's ears were so soft and fleshy. One day I was bothering him, I think, or he was just interested, and he jumped out the window of the car. We were in the Bois at the time, there is a road that runs through it, and he cut his eye on something. I never bit him on the ears again.

Chuck is still feeling bad. He wrote a poem today about a man praying before a pool of water. I felt today that I might be growing out of Chuck, growing away in the sense that I have been there where he is, and I'm tired of it, and I want to go away. Do you know what I mean? It's sad and I hope it isn't true. It was just that I shouldn't have been with him today.

July 15, 1969

HERBERT, SHEILA (our two new guests), Allan, and Charles slept peacefully on various floors and beds when I awoke Sunday morning. I fixed myself a quiet breakfast and slipped out into the hush of early Paris streets. The Métro was almost empty, a few children in their white clothes back from early mass, and a few others. The train finally came and I went again to avenue Georges V, and down the shaded street to the cathedral. It was still a few minutes before the service, so I waited on the bench nearby and watched Americans going to church, handsome couples and families and older people walking through the shade of the trees. Cars were scarce. An old French lady hung out her second-floor window and watched the Americans go by. I sat and had a cigarette as girls began to pass, and I nodded or just stared,

feeling fresh for the first time in a long while. Many of the
girls were beautiful, and I had brief, normal fantasies about
a few of them, and then went inside to confess my sins and
see the girls again.

I suppose they are beginning to know me there, the usher's
smiles are getting friendlier, and I am getting to know the
church again. I sat alone. The service began, and now I am
beginning to know the things you have to know by heart.
I only have to lower my head and mumble a few times during
the service. Two girls and two boys moved into the same
pew with me after the service had begun, probably French.
I showed them where things were in the hymnal, and then
listened to the sermon. A typically fascist statement about
the crime of putting "power into the hands of minorities"
and "so-called revolutionaries." Then the preacher proceeded to make outlandish statements about how the church
had not only invented all the good things in the world, like
love; not only that, but that without the church none of it
would have happened. I think I have a lot more respect for
human beings than that. But with that generalization, he
proceeded to shoot down anybody who had had anything
nasty to say about the church. I thought as I do sometimes
about walking out but then I thought of the usual shit such
as what would people say, and sat still.

When it was all over, and I do enjoy that service not
despite but because of the tradition, I followed one man
around who looked extremely familiar, finally caught him
and said:

"Excuse me, but I think I recognize you from somewhere."

He smiled nicely and looked down at me. "Well, maybe
you do. I'm Charlie Thompson."

"I'm Charlie Trueheart . . . Uh, are you in the Foreign Service?" I had really blown it, I had never laid eyes on him.

"No, I'm with a bank here. Why . . ."

"Well, I thought that's why I might have known you. You see my father . . ." and then we drifted apart.

Yesterday was Bastille Day and we watched the military parade from the seventh floor of the Pan American building on the Champs-Elysées. Exciting, lots of tanks and jeeps and trucks and soldiers. It was also terrifying that this is what people were cheering, but it was reassuring to see that also in the parade was the entire fire brigade in their asbestos suits with axes. Exhausted as we were, we all split up and went around and trickled back to the apartment by about 2 P.M. One by one we went to sleep in chairs and beds. I woke up at about six, cursing myself for not having called the Mannings as I had planned to, called them anyway and Mrs. said come over at seven for drinks. The others had gone off to see if they could eat at a free soup kitchen somewhere but Chuck and I were too silver-spooned. I put on some tomato soup and Chuck went into the john while I stood at the stove and stirred. In a moment I became aware of a presence in the room. I looked up. The front door had been open, and now there was a figure in the doorway, brown pants and white shirt, the light behind him bright enough so I had to adjust. He said nothing; it was Jeffrey. My index finger went to my lips and I ran over silently to him and pulled him out the door into the courtyard. I told him Chuck was in the john and that we would surprise him — just that afternoon he had had a dream about Jeffrey. (Chuck with Jeffrey and some friends from home on a road about to start hitchhiking. Chuck says good-bye energetically to his friends and then sort of waves quietly to Jeffrey. Walks off down the road to where Zeke is standing ready to go. They walk one hundred yards, and then Chuck breaks down crying and says he can't go, and walks back toward Jeffrey.)

"Chuck, I have a surprise for you."

From inside the stall: "What, did you find a finger in the soup?"

"Yes."

Chuck emerges and I am in the doorway. "What is it?"

"Come out here."

Out the door, looks around, Jeffrey: "Jesus Christ."

Reunion. Again, I am alone. But again, it only occurs to me in a flash. Post-occurrence, I like Jeffrey.

But I am not Chuck.

The apartment near the Etoile is plush. I ring. It has been a long time. Mrs. Manning, still young, pretty, though in her midforties at least, is at the door with the smile and the twinkling eyes which I had forgotten. We shake, I reach out and kiss her on the cheek, and the other one follows to my brief, adjusted surprise. They have lived in France for some time. The apartment is huge and very chic and with much of the same art that I had seen on white walls covered with geckos, furniture which had been left in storage during Saigon but which I vaguely remembered from old Paris days.

Jane, now twenty, emerges, grinning as always. We kiss, only once, and this time I surprised her. "Smooch," she says gleefully, and we sit down and smile at each other while Mrs. Manning looks on. Well, yes, it's been a while. Jane pulls out a cigarette. She has grown up, only now, for the first time, she is short and I am taller. She was always so big, but now she is small with breasts and legs and long blond hair, but still a girl the way she talks, giggling and warm and friendly and sometimes distant and sort of confused.

I pull out a cigarette. I have grown up too. What with our gin and tonics and our late dates and our cars, all new, all old, but instant reunion. Again, I am Charlie, and Chuck is not me, not this time.

I left after gin and tonics and met Jeffrey and Chuck under the Arc de Triomphe. We came home and met the others, turned on, and went to the Eiffel Tower to watch the fireworks. Somehow, the grouping happened to split as it had before many times, with Jeffrey, Chuck, and me together, and Al, Herbert, and Sheila together. We didn't see them again until we returned, but we went and stood under the tower. The fireworks were over when we got there, and I left Chuck and Jeffrey, perhaps as I should have. I looked at the people, searching again for someone to talk to, and saw two girls sitting nearby on chairs. I found a chair and sat and listened. They were American, as I had suspected. I was about to begin a conversation when a man, older, and a little boy, returned with drinks in paper cups. The man seemed about twenty-five, but I heard the little boy (about ten) call him Daddy, so he must have been older. He had long hair and a leather jacket — Davy Crockett — and the little boy looked dirty and poorly dressed. I gathered the *chutzpah* and began in French:

"Are you Americans?"

They also spoke in French: "Yes."

"Visiting here?"

"We've been here for six months. I am a playwright."

"I am an American too — from Washington."

"We're from California."

"Where do you live?"

"Montparnasse."

"I'm on the rue du Cherche-Midi."

"Oh, I see."

"As a matter of fact, I'm under contract from Houghton Mifflin for this summer. It's a journal, sort of . . . but it's different, because I don't have to depend on it. It's a whim, so it's not the same."

"Yes, you suddenly realize that you've done nothing for six months and you have to make a living."

"I'm sure that's true."

"Listen, why don't we talk in English?"

(In English.) "It was more fun the other way."

We chat further, and sometimes I stop and they go back together and talk among themselves. The little boy refers to his mother at home, so I gather that one of the girls there, about thirteen now that I see her up close, is also his daughter, and the other girl is older, maybe nineteen or twenty, and as I learn, English-Irish. Very hard to figure out what they are to one another, wives, mistresses, friends, sisters, brothers, and children, and the father with long hair, distant from any kind of father I have ever talked to — beautiful and tragic, exciting and confusing. We don't talk much more, except incidentally. The Irish girl rises and says:

"Well, then, bye-bye."

"Good-bye." I remain seated.

"We may see you again soon, maybe."

"I hope so." She is wearing no bra, and a loose lace blouse.

He: "Good-bye."

"Good-bye. Good luck." I mean it deeply, but he doesn't answer. He looks at me warily for a split second and then turns away.

It is after the long weekend, and the office is tired and irritable. We too are tired and irritable, and we talk about leaving the job because it is boring and restricting, but we will never do it. Chuck puzzling, going back toward self-righteousness, and I am his victim. We talk about the peeps we've been having, and the job, and he becomes miles and miles away. We remain silent. The other three fix us a beautiful spaghetti dinner on our return, a farewell for Herbert and Sheila on their way to Morocco, and they are all gone now, only Al reading and me typing.

It is hot and humid. Me, nude, and the typewriter. Thank you for listening.

July 16, 1969

I HAVE JUST eaten, and it is almost three hours since I have been home, three hours since I read your letter about John's car accident and Mike's death. We had heard about John through Chris, but we never knew it was so serious.

I know only that I am inexperienced in death, and that I have probably said that before in a context which I no longer remember, that perhaps everyone is experienced in life but no one is in death until one is faced with it. John is, maybe he knows it, maybe he doesn't. But to me, what has happened to him is near enough to death to be tragic. Because he is young, because I am young, then it is hard to believe, harder to cope with. All that keeps running through my mind is that I am with him as much as I can be, and that is not much because I am so far in every way, and also that I can never know how he feels. To say that it is a surprise and that it is still unimaginable is not saying much. I am bewildered at the magnitude.

That Mike is dead is more tragic. It is more moving and yet less so, because I did not know him either. What I know suddenly is that he is dead and that that could never happen to me, ever.

I chose to read your letter last. I always do because it will be the one I care most about. But the other three letters were from an unidentified woman who turned out to be my great-aunt. She had seen me only once three years ago and suddenly she sent me five dollars. Then Jennifer wrote for the first time this summer. A reassuring letter, different from most because it talked to me. She said, in her way, just what I wanted to hear but what I thought I wouldn't: we have a subtle friendship and she feels mild affection for me. She seldom says even that much. "I *do* miss you. Jennifer" was how she ended it, as if in rebuttal and I was defeated. *She does* miss me. And then a long, four-page, typed letter from my mother, one of the best letters she has written me, full of herself and how she feels about me, full of what is going on, full and beautiful. Absence makes the heart grow fonder, for both of us.

Then I read your letter, and the news. It was hard to know what to do, suppressing happiness at the other letters and yet feeling genuinely defeated. Still I can't tell you because I can't tell myself. It will be a week before you get this, I hope the most recent in a long line of letters that I have been writing, because you say that all you have gotten is postcards from places.

From my mother: "Your friend Sammy has a job downtown as a receptionist. He looks like a very nice boy considering his awful mother. I guess people say that about you. Which reminds me, I had a beautiful letter from Ted and Anne too. They both made me cry — I'm glad you weren't here."

July 17, 1969

I HAD ONE of the most terrifying and illuminating experiences tonight at the middle of our zonk. I began to catch Chuck on things he said, and pound him with questions deadly seriously until he sort of gave in or gave up. I would repeat some coy, subtle, double-entendre to bother the hell out of him, then repeat the cycles over and over again, ending with a few less subtle and absolutely unfelt statements about his personality. I commented about things he said and how much he meant of what he said and whether he was *really* this or that. Finally he broke down and started crying and I was still the astute, cold, pokerfaced interrogator who had just had another success.

The comments and the added presence of Al and Jeffrey made it sound like some Albee play, really horrible but exciting as hell. You see, I was both spectator and actor. I was getting a big bang about what I was able to pretend or act out. But that was it. It was a total act with statements that I had thought of that might well have been pertinent but nonetheless I didn't feel them at all — I was just using them in my little play. But he didn't know, and it turned into one of those Pirandello scenes where you don't even know whether you mean what you're saying or whether it's an act or the truth or both or neither. It was terrifying and it will remain. The hash had a lot to do with it, I'm sure, and I'm willing to classify it as a biggie in the annals of highs; not to make it seem any greater than it was, but to note that it happened. I am neither defensive nor offensive; it is simply by way of explanation, and you are my friend.

July 19, 1969

THE LAST TIME I wrote I imagine I was still slightly zonked, but I can't tell you to disregard what I said. Whatever it was, I think it has some bearing on what I'm going to say now, or somewhere in here.

The experience which I tried to recount, the anger and subtle enjoyment I was having starting the anger and keeping it up, is something that has bothered me, because I wanted it all to happen. I think I said a few journals beforehand that I am beginning to grow out of Chuck, and this was on my mind all week. For some reason, I think, I had to test him, I had to bring him out.

The morning after we were zonked he was saying merely that it had been an incredibly potent evening. I thought it was a lot more, not in the realm of the high itself, but in the realm of our relationship. At one point Chuck had come out of a mild catharsis, he lay back with his head tilted back so that none of us could see his face. He finally came to and looked around. We had all been silent, wondering if he was upset or not, and I knew that he was. He smiled and sheepishly said that he was really stoned. But for some reason I wouldn't let it go at that, and I continued to say things, things that I don't remember now at all, but things that pertained to him and that I wanted him to think I thought of him, which I really didn't. Then he broke up again and went back to my bed to lie there. A few seconds later Jeffrey got up and walked upstairs without saying a word. I had both succeeded and was crushed. I stood silent for a few seconds, smoking a cigarette. Al was watching me, I was on stage in a new play by Edward Albee. Chuck was silent behind the kiln, on my bed; I couldn't see him. I called upstairs, loudly and clearly: "Well, Jeff, do I come out the hero or the villain?"

That was the essence of it — I was hurting Chuck, but wasn't I also helping him, us? Jeffrey rose and came to the balcony and looked at me and said, "No it was just the strawberries. I'm sick from them."

I said OK and sat alone. I stood up and went to the kitchen. I overheard Al muttering something like ". . . just like I said . . ." I came back in and asked him what he meant, and he told me that it was all this self-analysis and looking at what you've said that makes things like that happen. It was the first time Al had ever been angry. That was good to see. Bastardly that for a second I looked at it that way, but it was good to see. He stopped for a minute, then added:

"I didn't like saying that."

"I'm glad you did, and you're right. But I was right too."

That was the end. We sat in silence and then it broke up and they went away.

It was meant to be cleansing, Ted, but I can never be sure. And I will never claim that it was right, but it was what I had to do, straight or stoned, for us, and it was easier to do stoned.

Something significant is happening here, and it is difficult
if not impossible to figure out, and it is me. In the past
twenty-four hours, and to a certain extent ever since the
other night, I am regarded differently. I don't think I am an
overly paranoid person, but I get the feeling that I am not
trusted — people are gracious and polite and friendly, but
jamais intime. It is a certain distance surrounding me (except for Al, who has kept with me and others a fixed distance
all along) a distance especially with Chuck.

With Chuck it is a very subtle consciousness that what we
say to one another is now stale and rusted — our friendship
existed first in a two-person situation, and second in a certain
(Exeter) environment. Our jokes and intimate little things
that all friends have, which usually change and continue,
now have worn out and it is as if I am groping for air. Chuck
has become critical of me, in a way which he denies but
in a way that he could only deny because he doesn't know it.
By the little anger he shows when he does deny it, then I
think there is some truth in what I say. As for me, I have
become critical of him, and I will deny it too, and know that
I am lying.

I can't say why all of this is happening. I feel it is more me
than him, and that I can see times when this has happened
before. When I become too demanding on my friends, and
especially with girls, it happens. It may be because Jeffrey
is here. When Chris was here, I may have taken it out on the
obvious scapegoat, but now perhaps I am getting right at
the root, and that is Chuck. Soon I will see that the root is
really me, and that's what I've got to look at. It is not

jealousy. It is a drive for personal power and attention that I have always needed. A drive for confidence. God knows I've got confidence, that I've got friends and attention, skill, and some power, but I am paranoid about that, very conservative in that I must fight for what I possess and can't afford to be generous with it. I am merely snatching in the wind for explanations and solutions. It will resolve.

Two Americans, hippies, were crouched in a Métro station today singing "Blowin' in the Wind."

July 20, 1969

TONIGHT SITTING having coffee after dinner we said whatever it is that I've been feeling — it came out somehow as a matter of course. We are lonely and often bored. It is an interesting comment on what we were saying at Exeter, how we would use our time once we were "free." Here we are in Paris, and while it is good for the soul, something is lacking. I guess that is the familiarity of being home. Behind being lonely is being homesick. On the surface what needs to be satisfied is a hunger for other people, and often, most often for me, it is a girl to talk with. Just that, and also someone to touch.

Today at church I saw a girl sitting a few pews behind me, beautiful, and I thought she might have been the girl from long ago who was supposed to be living in Paris. I wandered into the coffee hour and watched her sign the guest register and it was not she. I talked for a few minutes with a woman who used to be a friend of the family, then went outside and took my usual position on the bench on the avenue Georges

V. There I watch people as they come out of church and hope someone will stop and talk to me. Today, as always, no one did, but soon a man, black, came down to where I was, sat down, and we talked. Again an Albee play. He was eager to know all about me and not so eager to talk about himself. He said at first that he was a bum, had been for two years, in Paris from Ohio. But soon after I got to question him; he was not a bum but a student. We discussed my life and not much of his. He was very well educated, eloquent, and friendly. He wanted to know why I went to church. He said he thought it was a mockery. I told him I had spent enough time recently defending the church and that I was not about to do it again. It is something I find important in my life, I said, something good for someone who thought it was good, and something that I would never evangelize or force on anyone. The church is optional, and I have opted for it. That may not be an Episcopal thing to say or do, but I don't care. I think that I am a Christian, faithful to what may be. Absurd as it may seem, it is the hope that keeps me from jumping off the Eiffel Tower tomorrow.

But Alter Kidd (his name) said he would leave me so that I could have lunch, and he did. I had lunch and pursued my usual Sunday routine of buying a magazine and then walking around Paris and smiling at people I like. It is not much, really, but it is my day, the one Chuck sees when he says that is why he doesn't come to church anymore. He says it is the day I have to be alone, and he is right. I went to the Arc de Triomphe again and sat and read and a fag watched me from a few feet away, behind dark glasses.

The moon was a thin sliver tonight, and I admired it for

a few minutes and then knew that now things had changed.
Two men were there at that very minute, in awe of themselves and of the moon, perched on the sliver or lost in the
remaining darkness. It was not the same, it was as if I was
looking at New York City at night, coming into the harbor
on a boat. It was a light, immense, but suddenly not so distant, not so unreachable, human, and then soon, perhaps,
inhuman as a matter of course.

The moon shot is astounding, and more astounding I suppose for anyone who is older than I. It is something not to
be taken in stride, but something to be human and innocent
and full of wonder and to ooh and aah about.

July 21, 1969

TODAY WE have been congratulated by Frenchmen for our
success. *"Félicitations!"* A few minutes ago from the woman
across the courtyard, "We are proud of you." I said I was
proud too, thinking seconds later that I should have said
it is an international, a human, achievement. But one never
thinks of things like that at the right time. Besides, no matter
what you say, Armstrong and Aldrin and Collins are Americans. Those aren't reassuring words from a budding human-
itarian-diplomat, but they are basically honest. I am thrilled.

Today passed quickly — we worked, and during our lunch
hour we went to a café and watched the moon on television.
Really unbelievable, and we were congratulated for it. One
man who works in our office was in Paris when Lindbergh
landed, and he says he was amazed then. He keeps saying
that we are too young to understand the magnificence. He
is probably right. But as my father said in his characteristic

way in a letter I got today, "I must say it is hard to be blasé about this."

I may have said this before, but it has been going through my mind a lot today. I fear that this is the end of the Trueheart family. By the middle of autumn, we will all be gone in different directions for good. Distance and age and convenience will make it all end. It's really ridiculous to say, but it's true. It's as if I'm finally and inevitably "going out on my own," the time I always longed for, and it is uncomfortable and insecure. There are times when I think I will die if I don't get back to my bed or my bathtub or my refrigerator. All age-old symbols of childhood, but just because they are clichés doesn't mean they aren't very true.

We are quiet now. Jeffrey and Chuck are off walking. Jeffrey has joined the ranks as Thief, primarily because it fits the old rhyme, but also because he has stolen a few minor items, like a mattress, while in Paris. The mattress he walked off with today, and I'll never figure out how he did it.

July 23, 1969

LAST NIGHT we went out. I don't seem to talk about the days. The days are time wasted, time gone, time to think and become temporarily insane and work like a machine. A time, also, if I am kind and aware enough, to think about people who do what we do all their lives. But as much as one can learn, it is still painful and discouraging because I am helpless. I can do nothing but watch five Paris days go by every week. Nights are restful, peaceful, and sometimes drugged.

So last night we went out to the Palais de Chaillot across

from the Eiffel Tower. The fountains were open and spec-
tacular, so we took off our shoes and got a little wet and
watched tourists and laughed.

I left off for an hour to go have dinner with our neighbors
across the courtyard and it took more than an hour, two and a
half plus, all at the dinner table. She is an artist and he is a
lawyer and they had a lady friend with them. Two and a half
hours of solid French, no stops. Jeffrey, who speaks not a
word, sat in awe and despair the whole time while Chuck
and I chatted in what seemed like terrible French and Al
threw in a few comments now and then. They are terrific
people, at least the wife, who speaks some English and who
seemed to be the most aware of how we felt. There were two
tables and I was at one with monsieur and the lady friend
who talked between themselves the whole time with occa-
sional nods which I would answer with a knowing *oui, oui*.
They assumed that I understood everything they said. Of
course Madame watched me and all of us, smiling because
she knew how we felt. Much much wine and champagne
and a heated discussion on socialism which I only half-fol-
lowed, but pretended to be in complete agreement with both
of them. As it turned out their points of view were totally
opposed, so it must have looked strange. Nevertheless, they
were all very kind and I managed to follow the thread of the
conversation most of the way and to open and pour the wine
with grace and expertise. They dug us and we dug them.

I don't know if I told you about Alice, old Alice, near and
delicate like veneer. Charles Theodore received a passionate,
or should I say sensitive, letter from her the other day. I read

it with his permission. It was the kind of letter that I never got from her and wanted to so much. Alice is gone from me so it doesn't matter, but she met Chuck when he was visiting me for one weekend, less time than I had spent with her initially last Christmas. Now he gets the kind of letter that I wrote her at first and took shit for. Chuck, who is like me, became immediately interested — his word, a euphemism for infatuated — and wrote her and then wrote her again after last night to tell her about some things we read on the walls of the Palais de Chaillot. I have no editorial comment on the budding relationship. I just thought you might be interested. But may I predict right now that if Chuck is anything like me, which he is, and Alice is anything like she was, which she may not be, then it won't work.

The things we read last night. You ought to have them. I will try to translate: "Man is created without knowing it, just as he breathes. But the artist senses his own creation. His actions permeate his entire being. His pain, which he loves, fortifies him." The other one is, "It depends on who I meet whether I am a tomb or a treasure, whether I speak or am silent. It's up to you, friend. Do not enter without desire."

I finally received word from Webster Bull today, good words, appreciated and accepted if not absorbed. As much as he may have irritated me, I find I miss him incredibly. He didn't always irritate me, but things didn't jibe in the spring. His words: "I hope you didn't think I really resented you during the spring term. I *was* a bit put out by the journal, but only because it seemed to take an inordinate amount of your time and attention. I think we may have left too much unsaid; I really didn't know what you were thinking all term, and maybe I hid in Dramat House too much." And then some news which I want you to hear not because you are interested or because you particularly like Webster Bull, but because I like his letter. Whether you like him or not I don't know. I think he secretly liked you but was afraid of Deacon Power.

> Life here is what they call a real experience. Some flashes: a few screaming queers who keep to themselves, and a number of hard-core fags, all making opening night parties resemble *The Boys in the Band.* On the verge of my first dick. (How's that for a little superficial ego-tripping, eh Chuck?) A lot of nice people who really seem to know what they're doing, although they spend a little too much time discussing: [And then he has a half-page drawing, ornate and gaudy, of the words "The Theater" plus "in all its glory."] Minimal drugs. A beautiful beach. A lot of work building scenery in the shop which is really nice when you find that you can really work with your hands, something I haven't done for quite a while. And lots more (as they say).

In closing, he writes, "With deep warmth, respect, and all, Web. P.S. God, I miss you guys."

He is a powerful and exciting person and I miss him no end.

July 26, 1969

FINALLY I arrive at the written word after many days when it was put off for other, unjudged moments of ecstasy and occupation. I have now returned to the again unjudged state of writing to you, a state that comes and goes and is hard to enter and easy to leave.

Last night after light intoxication I spoke at length with

Chuck about myself. What is Alice like, he asked, and I said
that perhaps I shouldn't answer. He said I was right, but
then I went ahead and told him what she and I were like.
The only really good time was that weekend when you drove
us down to Boston and we talked and talked and then
touched in the back seat coming back up, as Sarah stole
glances over the front seat and then sat frozen in fear
and embarrassment. You snorted and chuckled and I was
ashamed. Imagine, doing that sitting behind a man of the
cloth. I suppose I knew that you were more, or to throw out
the quantitative judgment, something else. Chuck said that
to him our relationship had seemed sterile — we hadn't
touched. Yes, that is true, but for me it is always true, it
seems. Jennifer in her recent letter: "Right after you left
people began hounding me to search my soul and release it
into 'meaningful relationships' or something. I think I do,
but they just don't manifest themselves in physical commitments — and I regret that but it won't be solved by self-
analysis. Will it? (*Tell me.*)"

Then we continued to talk and at one point Chuck said to
me that a lot of his friends seemed alike in many ways, but
that I was absolutely unique. I pressed him for more. In a
way, I wanted him to criticize rather than just say this is you
and this is me. So he said that I was one of the most intense
people he knew. What does intense mean? He said I was
intense like old people were, nervous. I think he is right, but
that was what I was worried he would say.

One of the standard jokes in Studio D is my worrying. It
is true, and I think it has been for at least three or four years.
I spend a great part of the day worrying about myself and
us and what we are going to do and what we have done, and

then try to solve things. But always. Being miles away from where I can do anything about it, both geographically and spiritually, it is now intensified. I mean everything.

I suppose you have figured this out about me by now, and it is true. What I told Chuck last night was that I do it so that whatever makes up my life remains as crystal clear as possible, that of course it never does but it is good and re-assuring and time-consuming to think that I have tried to make it clear. I run problems and worries and anxieties and every kind of possibility through my head constantly to keep everything about my life in touch. Then Chuck said that I must be miserable, that I couldn't be having a good time here. He's right, but I'm not having any worse a time here than anywhere else. I only have good times in fantasies and epiphanies — like last night, when my mind was working at full force and digesting and spewing. I have become ex-tremely talkative here, maybe again to fill up time and space, maybe also because I worry that no one is listening.

The rest is flashes. Chuck is writing poetry. We sat with a group of French and all-nations young people (I hate that phrase with a passion. It sounds like someone wanted to say long-haired communist faggots but was too polite) on the tip of the Ile de la Cité. Again I felt alone. No one really knew each other. I mean, we didn't know them and they were together and they sang songs so we were able to sit in. But for me it was sad because I wasn't a part of it, only sitting in and trying and wishing. Al ran into someone who was selling speed. The group got larger and larger after about an hour, so I sensed that there were too many young people and too many drugs, which may have been wrong and fascistic to think, but I did, so I decided to leave. Chuck followed and Al stayed and sure enough there was a minor bust about fifteen minutes later. I missed the action, but I really had to take a whiz.

I can't seem to write about the office. Parts of it are worth retelling, parts are things I won't forget, but they seem foreign and disturbing when I want to write about them. I am a different person when I am there, and we all are, but the concept of being a "different person" is wedged to begin with. Friday when one of the secretaries asked me if Al was always a clown, I said rather profoundly, even in French, and even with a hint of editorial comment, "We are very different people at the office." Al immediately turned to me and said, "Tu ne me connais pas." You don't know me. I was shocked, but I said, sighing, "Yes, that's true." Al, yes it's true, I don't know you. I think *you* know you, but no one else does. Let the sunshine in.

July 27, 1969

DEAREST TED: At this moment this is addressed to you, as it always is, but now in name.

Sunday. My day, the Sabbath, when God rested. Why do we worship Him on the day He rested? I would never be able to evangelize from the pulpit of the American cathedral in Paris. I go every Sunday and there is little that is friendly or warm there. And at what point in my adolescent life do I have the balls to accost someone and say what I feel? I like the way you look. I am lonely. Talk to me. Take me out. Do me a favor. I'm interesting too. Is this done? Does it cut any shit whether it is done or not?

I took the train to Versailles after lunch to visit the *Palais*. It slowly came back to me once I got off the train what Versailles was like. The grand avenue that leads up to the golden gates of the palace grounds, cobblestones, heat, people making a pilgrimage to what they might have had if they had been lucky and born four hundred years ago. I was sweating, perspiring under the sun that I suppose gave the king his name. Inside it was cool — and free because it was Sunday and I am a student. I began a little tour through hundreds of rooms with paintings of people who really don't interest me, paintings of Versailles long ago, which for some reason do interest me. My eyes as usual kept an ever alert watch for the young ladies who also toured the rooms. My eyes met with some who were beautiful but nothing more. I proceeded upstairs and was pursuing a rather perverted habit I have picked up recently for reasons that have already become evident, a habit of, when in large crowds, fondling the buttocks of young ladies as I push by in the crowd. Yes, well, that's what I was doing in one of the most beautiful and historic edifices in the world. I will probably remember it for that. I might, but I think I may remember it for something else, for a beautiful girl. An anticlimax, perhaps, but yes, it's true. I wish I had the power to describe in words what she was like, but I can only describe my reactions and actions. Slim, light, rosy cheeked, wrinkled lips, but more than that, and that says nothing: simplicity, serenity, grace, depth. Our eyes met several times as they usually do when one of two people is looking. And once I even smiled, but that was it. I followed her around some of the rooms just watching. She was with her little sister and she was accosted by some

French guys who did the usual moves for picking up a foreign girl — I'm not sure whether she was American or English. I felt slightly disappointed that I had been without balls and had let them do their thing, but it is always easier to follow and be a pervert. She looked innocent with them, kindly and mildly responding to their jokes, and soon they all went outside. I thought they might sit down on some steps so I did and watched. Alas, they walked away toward the gardens and I thought I might find her later. I went back and walked around, and sat for two hours in one spot thinking that she would surely come by, and what would I say and what would we do and how close would we become, but nothing, really nothing, just me thinking what if.

It is like that, Ted, not just right now, not just in Europe, but always. Too vain and too proud to try to pick someone up, too shy to say anything, and then secretly loving the misery that follows. But I don't. I hate it. Jennifer and Bob Dylan, you are wrong. I am litle boy blue, I do brag of my misery; but it is because misery is what I have, misery alone, in the realm of reality, and everything else, happy-ness included, is in the realm of fantasy. And real or fantastic, I do take myself too seriously, but only because there is no humor in my real existence. Good Christ, I even thought, this girl might be waiting at the station, and then on the train, and then back in Paris. In Paris — can you imagine? — people waiting for me with arms and tears and love right here in my own fucking apartment?

You see, Chuck, you see, all of you, I am trying very hard to bring what I want and need into my life. But it is not easy. I am not willing, anyone, to think that life is a joke. I must take, no matter how absurd, my existence as something important, by the very word *vital*, the most vital thing I have. I hope one day I can live in some sort of anti-misery. But I expect too much. I want to expect the ultimate in my fantasies, otherwise I will settle for less. That is all. That is my last will and testament, that is what I am going to be, and nothing will change it, not even the ultimate. But for God's sake, love me for trying hard.

July 29, 1969

I HAD THE time and the energy to write you last night but there was no subject matter. Tonight, again, there is no subject matter, and I am writing anyway. I have only little things to report. I have thought much and felt much but nothing I haven't before, nothing that I am interested in writing about.

In six months I may wonder how I could ever have felt this way. So much already seems unreal. Could I have ever felt love for any of the people I really did? Could I ever have been angry or disgusted by Mel or Peter or Webster when I miss them so much right now? Do they have any faults at all? Damn it all, someone said it before me — absence makes the heart grow fonder. And absence makes Trueheart founder. A real shaking of the foundations.

Ted, so much goes through my head that it is often unbearable. So much longing for what I don't have and so much hating of what I do, and so much escape into what was never, is not, and never will be. Is it youth, me, or life? That is the essential question I've got to answer. That is really, fucking, *it*.

July 31, 1969

FRUSTRATED THAT these words, whatever they may be, will not reach you until Monday or Tuesday, and all the more so because I am feeling so much from your letter. I will now try to respond to some of the wisest and warmest words I have heard in a long time, perhaps since your letter received early this month, the one you said you wished you had made a copy of. I would be organized to go through your letter point by point but I cannot. I would get carried away, so I might as well begin carried away.

I don't know how birthdays are for you, or for anyone as he gets older. I know that for my parents it is made to be more than it is because Josh and I are around. And I also know that birthdays have meant less and less to me in the past few years. It used to be that I could remember every birthday I had and which one it was, but I can no longer do that. At any rate, I hope you had a happy birthday, and if you were as moved by man on the moon as I then it must have been. If the girls were happy, all four of them, then you were, and that, I suppose, is what it's all about.

But I am really shilly-shallying to talk about that. It is important but it is not what moved me about your letter. What did move me were the few words in your long passage on the win-lose game.

Chuck: I thought first that I had been able to put aside, for the sake of discussion, the fact that we were stoned that night. But that is neither here nor there. We were, we have been, we will be. It is not happy, and I think about it much before and after, and often during, and you are a part of that much. It is not because I don't love or respect you that I can still go into it, it is inexplicable. It is not a matter of going along with the guys. We are careful about that. No, it is not every night.

But back to Chuck: I did not win, I did not lose. It was a game, yes; but that I knew it made it different. "You won with Harris on that zonked evening . . . but Jeffrey saw and so did you that to win was in fact to lose, and so it is the other way around." The tragedy was that Chuck did not know it was being played. That was my loss, no question. I had something to say that I couldn't say except in a game (zonked or straight) and I said it. I play a game, the game you talk about, often, and maybe as your letter hints, always. You are more than right, you are kind to say "What's the point?" There is no point, but it is *in* me and I wish it would go. I knew that night that I was fucking around, I knew it and continued because it was stimulating. It was very unkind, and yet at the time I thought it might be cleansing. It was. So I was not really playing it because I knew it was not real, I knew it was something out of Albee. Yet now I am becoming aware that I play it always, and more frightening, that I have played it and you have noticed it. "The game can be won, and it is very tempting, but what's the point? — and that is no 'negoism,' in fact quite the opposite." That is what shocks, what moves, that is the part I'm talking about. It is only frightening because you say it in passing, as if I know what you mean. Do I?

And then the trust: my first reaction is to sigh and say yes I have noticed it. People have said I am a conniver and a politician, and I am, but I don't want to be. It is maybe because never, when I was young, did I have many friends. I felt I needed something to prove myself; something to maneuver with and get myself somewhere. That may still be here. I sense it is. I think you do too. My second reaction is to be angry, but that goes quickly. I think that you and a very few other people know me well enough to trust me, as you said, and the others want to but are never sure. Still others won't try. It makes me feel good, and more, when you wrote: "All of which says to me, when a person doesn't trust someone like you, it says more about that person's inability to look at and be honest about themselves, which is what I feel when I hear such a comment . . ." Yet I am responsible, and whether I have to go out of my way to make someone trust me doesn't matter, whether they do trust me or not does matter.

Ted, is feeling like that playing the game?

Doctor and Mrs. Scheer came last night and took all of us out to dinner. They made me think of Peter. Just as Chuck said I was a product of my family, Peter is absolutely and perfectly so. In the Bois de Boulogne, they and I eating a late afternoon picnic before returning to Studio D, Mrs. Scheer said, "I think Peter feels closer to you than anyone else." I said that I thought that had always been true but we had never said so, we had never needed to say it out loud. They took us out to dinner and we wandered, the six of us, up and down the banks of the Seine and into the Algerian restaurant section for *couscous*. Four adolescents showing a part of Paris to two adults. Something about us that, besides all our troubles and unhappiness and joy, we were proud of.

In the restaurant I took it upon myself to do the ordering. Toward the end we decided on getting some more sauce and I said that I would ask for it. Suddenly Chuck looked up at

me and said, "Yeah, would you do that for us, Charlie?" Yes,
despite my affection for the Scheers, despite the fact that I
spoke French very well, despite everything — that I was
playing the game, wanted to impress — I was proud to do it.
I might have showed up my friends, and especially Chuck,
whom it hurt the most, maybe for the very reason that he too
plays the game with me. I don't know, these are only
thoughts, and again I don't know much about the nature of
the game. But I might have been playing it *for* someone, and
for someone else, Peter, driving across the Bad Lands. I
might have been proud, young, and eager to show my affection and who I was, now, here.

August 2, 1969

BEFORE I COULD stop the world, or even change it, it became
August. Always August is climactic, and always it is the
beginning of the end. On August 1–2, 1966, I had a love
affair on a beach in South Carolina. From early August last
year I have a poor poem called "night of august eight." I
wrote a lot of poetry last August.

After I wrote you last Thursday, I sat down and had a
cigarette in the "living room" and asked Chuck to join me.
Then I said that I wanted to talk to him and to read your
letter to him. So we went out to a café and I read it to him,
and we talked to one another for the first time in a long while.
What came out of our talk was a clarification of what happened that night. A few things surprised me. The main thing
was that Chuck had been so totally aware of what was going
on and of everything I said.

I don't want to make a huge issue of that evening, it doesn't deserve it. We talked about trust, and he said that what had bothered him all summer was this, these words. He said that that very night, Thursday last, I had been sitting at the dinner table, and suddenly I jumped up, rushed over and started typing. Jeffrey said to Chuck, "How does he do it?" and Chuck replied, "He can because he's been thinking for two days what he's going to say." Now I don't think that's really true, nor was it true last spring when Webster said it to me. But that is the way they see it.

Then we talked about Al, and then about our respective outlooks on friendship, which turned out to be practically identical. We both demand an expressed recognition of the state of the relationship; we can't stand not to have someone say that he or she (especially she) is digging a certain thing if that is the case. It is a fear of saying even that that makes it so hard for Jennifer and me. She holds that she can't say she loves me because if the next day she didn't, she would have lied.

To be young, isn't it not to have to be sure? Isn't it the freedom and ease of not having to be certain and the joy of being almost always confused? And hoping that once in a while you're not? And if not, fine, if so, good?

This whole thing sounds like a doctoral thesis, it is so dry, but that must be the state of my mind right now.

Chuck got a letter from Alice today which I read at his urging, and which I set down on the coffee table with no comment. It was, I hate to say, and don't to Chuck, the kind of letter that would have swept me off my feet about six or eight months ago, but which I can see through now. I can see Alice clearly now, and Chuck too. That is not to say I am looking through shells, but just more clearly at personalities.

For the thoughts which Alice expresses were those that finally turned me off to her because I could no longer believe them to be honest thoughts: Running through the rain with a raindrop on my nose, yes, living life, smilingly, wishing I could be in Paris with you, and yet, things are so tender, like little children, happy, Alice.

That is the way it is with her. Not always, but just enough to make me think she was somewhere else, and that she knew she wasn't but wanted to be. What is more frightening is to think Chuck is feeling the same way. I often get the impression he is, but he has also said to me specifically that he can't believe that she believes it. But now my hunch is that he writes her the same way, and says the same things because he would like it to be that way, with her and with everybody, a life without anger and trouble and worries. That's Alice's spell. I don't think I would want it to be that way. Running with a raindrop on your nose can only go so far.

August 3, 1969

WE DID NOTHING last night but sit around and rap about youth. Again, Chuck and I ate out; Jeffrey is out with a girl friend and Al is in Switzerland. We talked about how happiness is always in the mind but never when it's happening; we listened to the tunes on the restaurant's jukebox that made me think of Johanna and then we walked back. I dozed off in a huff because something had grated. I was homesick. Then Jeffrey called and asked if we wanted to go out with some girls. It was like Chuck had been brought back to life from a mood of quiet serenity to suddenly exuberant serenity, like his oxygen had been restored. Jeffrey had called. I must

be awfully jealous to be thinking these things, but it isn't that.
I really do like Jeffrey.

These damn girls are coming any minute so I have to type
like a bastard. I didn't do anything else except buy a *News-
week* as I do every Sunday and read under the Arc de
Triomphe. There were no fantasies and not even any fags
staring at me. The fantasies seem to have gone this Sunday,
my time alone might almost have been spent *with* someone.
I returned early and sat with Tom Shepherd for a few hours
(we ran into him yesterday at the Orangerie), as he had
come over to use my big blue writing machine to change
some numbers on his motorcycle insurance. We talked.
Again he is one of those people you never knew at all and
wish you had. He was interesting and likable and radical in
the way I would like to be: carefree and raising some hell and
once the hell is raised, for a good cause mind you, once it is
raised, going back to being your regular Joe Fascist.

August 8, 1969

WHAT COULD I have said on a postcard from Cannes? Only
that I was enjoying myself. What can I say now that I have
gone and returned? Again, I enjoyed myself.

Eve of departure: I wrote you and mailed the letter, and
sat quietly with Chuck for a long while, and then Jeffrey
came with his girls. I decided to begin drinking because for
some reason I feared that the experience would be painful.
So I had three gins and orange juice, and then proceeded to
enjoy myself when they came over. Nice, simple girls from a
school in Delaware, and Chuck was miserable. I couldn't
understand what was really going on, except that as I said,

Chuck was miserable, and he had one of his moments when we were walking over to where the girls were staying. He stopped and clutched his hands together in front of his face and sobbed. Those moments have lost their effect on me because I can't understand why he is feeling the way he is. It is alien to what I feel, and therefore I see it as lacking reality. He said later that he realized he wanted to go, run away from those girls, but that he couldn't, his mind wouldn't let him. He was frightened by the power of his intellect. It was Chuck's last night with Jeffrey, and he was sad because it wasn't what it might have been. I went to bed when we got home and the two of them sat up and talked late, later than it already was, and I could only imagine it as one of those sighing, smiling talks where all is good and beautiful. Jeffrey is realistic and not like that, just a very composed person. I only feel that the composure is forced, or hiding something else, when I see it in Chuck. But I love Chuck. We had a good time together last week, and there is nothing I should be bothered by, except my own reactions to a very well-living person.

As a result of our late night, we overslept and woke up at eight-thirty to catch a nine o'clock plane. Chuck had said the night before that he never really wanted to go on the trip and leave Jeffrey. I was deeply suspicious that he didn't want to make the plane. Willy-nilly, we did, a small private jet which flew us exhausted to the Côte d'Azur. The airport in Cannes is like something in a movie — a small seaside airstrip with palm trees, something in the Brazilian hinterland where natives pick you up zebra back or something. We walked toward town, saw a gas station renting motorbikes, and suddenly the entire jaunt was made. We chose our little machines and for the next four days, with swims and meals in between, zoomed up and down the coast like international jet set Hell's Angels on less than potent machines. We found a quaint little hotel when we got to town. The Hôtel de Strasbourg, small, breakfast on the terrace. However, we stayed *under* the hotel, in a dungeon (called euphemistically a "dormitory") with no light, no john, no shower, no sheets, just rows of bunks. It looked like a Civil War hospital, with sweating, snoring male bodies lying crumpled on filthy mattresses, yellow, damp sheets twisted obscenely around their legs. This was home for the next four nights, and I had my sunglasses, cracked as they were, stolen by one of the demented cretin onanists that made the cellar his year-round habitat, sleeping, hagging it, whacking it during the day — although you couldn't tell day from night as there are no windows — and prowling around during the night groping into people's pockets and presumably into people's beds. Chuck says I exaggerate, but that was the way I felt.

What was fun was to walk, looking like we did, through the terrace where the "guests" of the hotel ate their meals. That was the only way to get out of the dungeon, through the breakfasting French aristocrats, who would yank their little dachshunds toward them and look the other way when we walked by.

The night before the night before we left, we had dinner at a restaurant in a town called Théoule, and then proceeded further west on our Freudian machines. In about ten minutes we passed two Americans, a boy and a girl. We went past them and I said to Chuck that they looked like Americans and that we should stop and talk. This we did, pulled over, waited, and they finally came up to us and we struck up a conversation. It is hard to know what really happened, whether they were as fantastic as they seemed; but we talked there, at the side of the road on a hillside, until one in the morning as if we had been best friends for ages. We offered them a peep, and then talked for many hours, deciding that if we had recorded the meeting from start to finish, and sold it as a play, we would have made a million. They were great people, and more than that, they filled a gap for us, and we for them. Their freshness was beautiful. The circumstances made it all the more amazing, in the road like that.

We got in last night to see Al, happier than I've ever seen him, returning to what is now home, really home, with sheets and a chair and refrigerator.

And this morning a strange, sad letter from Puck, who was stoned at Sequoia Park when he wrote it.

. . . Thus far the summer has been a strange one and very different from Exeter although I am trying constantly to re-create some type of Exeter security, and always finding myself ultimately questioning the Rev's concept of reality at Exeter. I was very depressed about John and Mike and found all my memories of Gleason sermons and Judy Collins songs of little comfort. I heard a few words from Louie Pressman implying the same kind of simplistic emotional response. Mike is dead and John's life is fucked and the combined philosophies of Kierkegaard, the Rev, Dean Bob, and Bucky Bruce aren't going to change that.

I thought Linda was pregnant but she had her period when the Apollo 11 landed. That was a very frightening time of little sleep and numes haggars when I was faced with the very lucid reality of three irreparably ruined lives and numerous others made miserable. Compared with that, getting shot down at Harvard or put on pros or kicked out means relatively little. The damage then is inflicted only really on yourself and can be overcome.

I think he has missed the point, Ted, but he spoke and I hear his every word. I'm going to write him and respond, and I'm not even sure how much of what he says he believes or was even aware of saying. The last line of the first paragraph is what bothers me and what I think really misses the boat. As much as neither of us likes criticism, and I take this as personally as you will, I think first that he was trying to tell me something. My response is either that I am blind or he is very very wrong. I thought you should hear it.

August 10, 1969

I WRITE THIS now in a haste that is warranted only by the fact that I am tired and/or the fact that soon we will have company. Though it is eleven-thirty, this has become not unusual. Last night, Bill Windsor brought over the majority of his travel group for what was the first orgiastic get-together that I have ever hosted with the possible exception of the little bacchanalian fest I gave with friend Casey last Christmas in Washington, and which you have heard so much about.

Chuck was going to an Ionesco play; Bill and his group were going out to dinner; and Al and I were to prepare for the entire group to come over at eleven, some twenty strong. So after much hassling and exchange of money and telephone calls and argument, Al and I went out and bought wine at a local store, returned and set things up. We thought we might

have seemed strange and had visions of shopkeepers saying
heh heh so yoo are going to have a partee, heh heh, but no
they didn't flinch as we asked for ten liter bottles. We met
Bill at eight-thirty at his little restaurant and completed plans
for the evening. Then we wandered down to dope alley and
looked for our friend Tintin, a major hashish dealer in
Paris, but there were many policemen and little gumption.
Promptly at eleven-thirty, all eighteen guests arrived. They
sat all over the room and floor and we drank wine and
chatted. Five or six male and female jock friends of Mickey
from Dartmouth (we met some time ago during the first
days) came soon after. Now we were about twenty-five in
our apartment. Much talk and wine and then many left because the last Métro was at 1 A.M. Eight remained: Mickey,
Jean, Bill, Chuck, Al, two girls, and me, Jean being Bill's love
and the object of Mickey's crude but fun-loving lust for that
evening. We had a peep together and Bill did a communion
with bread and wine. We whispered late into the night with
music, with (as Scheer says) numes haggars, and finally
retired at three-thirty with our guests asleep all over the
apartment. This morning at seven-thirty, who should appear
at the door but Indian Chief — Chris — from four weeks of
traveling and an ego fit to burst. All of us were up and
running around by nine, talking, picking ourselves up and
cleaning the ashes and bottles and bread from all over the
floor, and then I departed faithfully to church.

There I suddenly turned around and saw Mr. Manning, my
godfather, who stood with me some twelve years ago not
ten yards from where I was and became my godfather. The
final candle was out. I felt exhilarated by the final hymn
as I perpetually am; I stood out in the aisle and turned

toward him, smiling. He gave me a pleasant smile and I
continued to smile and he did a proverbial double take.

He: "Is that you?"

"Yes it is."

(Arm around me.) "Well, I'll be damned." (Thick Southern accent; I had forgotten.) "It's great to see you."

"It's great to see you too."

We talked and I was introduced to all the people I had
been secretly watching for all these damned Sundays. He
told the true story about me being baptized: Manning said
to me, are you scared of being baptized, and there was an
old man with a long white beard being baptized with me, so I
responded, no, not with Santa Claus here with me. They
have never forgotten it. What do you say except I am flat-
tered and charmed to hear it and I too remember things,
things that were unimportant but made impressions. I stood
aside as he talked to people, tried to be young and poised, but
didn't succeed. Does it matter? Yes, it does, no matter what
I can be told, yes it does. He drove me to the Métro and had
to go so I came home.

You are always here in me, a conscience, but that is too
strict a word, perhaps a part is better, a part of everything I
think and do. Maybe you have lost some respect or trust, I
don't know and I am not searching for assurances, but I am
living a life now (as I think I always have) of which I am
proud and will defend it if I have to. I don't have to with
you, so I won't here. What I must do is tell you about it and
present it to you, and most of all, let you know and see that
your words never leave me, none ever have. I may be blind
to many things, but what I see I never ignore.

✸

August 12, 1969

I JOINED the others Sunday night, not in any inebriation but
in quiet conversation. The decision was made for everyone
to sleep here, ten people in all, and I crawled into bed. Soon
after Jean crawled in with me, and we began to sleep. Just
as the night before, someone was snoring — Mickey I think,
though he denies it — and his sleeping sound made us laugh
and chatter. Chris was on a mattress with a girl, Chuck in
his bed with someone else, I think, and the others sprawled
around. It was hot, and I was, though practically naked, also
sweating. An hour later, Jean said damn it and sat up and
removed her shirt to reveal a beautiful body. After more talk,
whispers between naked strangers who had never really seen
each other's faces because it was so dark, here in bed and
before, we slept soundly and peacefully. Perhaps for the first
time I can say I went to bed with a beautiful girl; but it was
far more delicate than that.

Last night, Chuck and I went out to dinner because when
we returned from work there was no food, and all our guests
had left the place upside down. It didn't matter because
sometimes it's like cleaning up your own soul, perhaps an
excuse or a projection of what you would like to do, to clean
the apartment from top to bottom and then leave it intact
for a few hours while you rest over a whole meal and are
waited on. We returned after dinner and Al had returned
from Versailles. We waited, perhaps for the group tour to
come over. Mickey came, and a few others. We sat quietly,
and I wrote Puck, and Chuck wrote Alice, and we spoke.
I curled up on a mattress on the floor and had one of those

non-night sleeps where you half-sleep and sweat and vaguely hear conversation in the room and pretend you don't and cut off what you don't want to hear, because you are warm in your position and don't want to move. Someone mentioned yogurt and that made me rise to have a carton of it. It was midnight and we had stayed up too late and no one had come.

I am sipping a Coca-Cola and smoking one of the expensive cigars left by the Scheers when they were here. Allan is reading Che Guevara and Charles is writing his mother. The time is together and peaceful and welcome; it has been a long time since it has been so. We have just eaten a delicious dinner with our boss; and we expect the group again for a going away party at eleven. Nothing could be better for an evening: a little refinement, conversation, and good food, a little homebody living, and writing to loved ones and reading. Then the enjoyable debauchery.

The summer closes soon. It will be sad and missed, but not for long. It will never be remembered as it really was. It was never seen before as now. And even now it is rarely, only momentarily, seen as it really is, and even then there is always doubt. That's not just summertime, either.

Now is one of those rare times when I am finished with the letter but I don't want to go away. I want to explore inside some more to see what else I can scrape out for you. But there is a conflict, that I don't want to scrape out too much because it would be like drinking on an empty stomach when my life continues.

The letter, sealed and mailed.

✲

August 13, 1969

Out of the blue (intended) me: "I'm desperate to go back
to the States. I have nothing to go back to, but it's nice to
have your own room, your own bed, where you can be alone
and stop thinking, stop having to worry about what you're
doing. I guess it's never really like that, but that's the way I
see it."

Allan, across the dinner table, dark, evening, the eve of
our last day of work, one week from our return, over goulash
and rice: "An unexamined life is not worth living, and an
examined one is impossible to live."

Pause. Truth. Striking home.

And Chuck: "That's nice." In his incomparable fashion
with the dreamy look of pleasure and serenity.

Again it all passed too quickly, but last night I spent one
of the most miserable nights of my life. I thought — in the
darkness sometimes and in the light and sound of people
talking a few yards away on the other side of the kiln —
seriously, I think, of going home that very instant, of getting
away, and equally seriously but less vividly, of suicide. For
the first time in a long time. The question is why. The question is that after the letter full of hope and peace last night,
how the torment could have occurred, the hate and misery
could have taken my being over for so long, so profoundly.

After I wrote, I rested in my clothes on my bed, past
eleven, past twelve, past one, waking up occasionally to say
a few words to Al who slept in a chair by the door, waiting,
as I was and Chuck had given up doing, for Bill and his
friends. Finally, after one, three girls arrived through the

door, including Jean. I rose from my bed, rather tired, thinking vaguely and madly and hotly of the fact that twenty minutes before they had arrived, I had listened to and refused to partake in a conversation and eventual taking of speed by Al and some guy from NYC.

They weren't sure what they were taking — "How many should we take?" "I don't know what it is" — discussing past drug experiences with a certain pride which I can excuse. I was worried and mad because they were going to take pills about whose substance they were totally ignorant. The NYC stranger, who was the tempter, with whom I was now angry and disgusted, said, "Wouldn't it be freaky if it was acid?" Al laughed and said, "Yeah." And they took the pills. I thought for a while, and didn't know what to do. Then I got up and walked out to them (this was about midnight) and sort of stood there. NYC stranger said, "Do you want some speed? I have plenty of it." And I said no, and he said OK. Again, I was compelled to say more, so I said I didn't take speed, and he said it wouldn't hurt me. I said I was sure it wouldn't, but that I just didn't feel like it. Then dumbly, because I felt vegetable-like standing there and watching them, expecting them I suppose to explode or something, I walked back to my bed and rested and listened to them talk for about thirty minutes, and then got up again, after much conflict and said to them in a rather prepared way, "Look, I don't want to seem a prude, and I don't know anything about speed, but I just . . . well, I wanted to tell you to be careful." A couple of confused looks, and then mumbles of oh it's OK. I stared at them again, very tired, and went back to bed.

An hour later, not having really slept at all, just having sat and thought and listened to them talking — Chuck was asleep or resting as I was, I will never know which — the people, the three girls, walked in. I rose, as I said, and went out and sat with them for a cigarette. Jean went upstairs and was there for a few minutes. When I went up to see what she was doing, there she was on Chuck's bed giving him a back rub. "Is he asleep?" "I don't know." I laughed and went back downstairs. I sat in a chair as the others talked. I had wanted to get to know one girl, but now, now that it was all there in front of me, now that I was watching it all detached and analytical, with no one, absolutely no one, looking at me or saying a word to me, now she was less appealing. The NYC stranger was even less tolerable because he was talking as he sped. I was quiet and tired, and I began to look off into space: more whispers from one of my closest friends and the girl who had slept with me two nights before from upstairs. Chuck was talking serenely and religiously to her, really nice, full, peaceful were his words, the same Chuck that for a still and really inexplicable reason bothers the hell out of me. I was starting to shit on myself because I was lonely and mad and worried and jealous for every possible reason. After about an hour and a half, I said, "I'm going to bed," and got very little response. Worse, half an hour later, one girl said "Oh, did he go back there? I didn't even notice." An hour later, I was listening to all three conversations: the constant rapping of the NYC stranger and one girl, the hesitant dialogue of Al and the other, and the exchanged sweet nothings of Chuck and Jean upstairs replete with pregnant and mysterious sighing pauses. Listening for when Chuck, not having even noticed that I had gone and been silent for an hour and practically so all night, realized that I had gone to bed, listening until three when everyone left (but me and

Chuck and Jean upstairs) full of good-byes, for which I sat up and nodded and said various meaningless things.

Then in the final darkness I turned in my sweaty sheets. I thought the most horrible and manic depressive thoughts of my life, full of hate and lacking in any kind of hope or goodness. That is what I can't explain. It was a combination of every event and person there that evening, and I suppose implicitly in contrast to such nice expectations, stupid or fantastic as they may have been. I finally fell asleep at about five-thirty and woke at seven when Chuck called. I rose and made a little breakfast while the other two laughed upstairs, together in the shower. I was wallowing in a misery and a frustration unimaginable, still inexplicable, but perhaps evident tomorrow or even now for you. At seven-thirty, one half-hour before we usually had to leave for work, I rose from the breakfast table and said, offering my hand to Jean, "It was charming to have known you." I meant it exactly as that: I was charmed by her, nothing more or less. She gave me a quizzical, half-laughing look. Chuck was shocked, and I started away.

"Where are you going?"

"To work."

"But . . . now?"

"Yes, now."

And I left.

Chuck and I had lunch together at a café. I told him pretty much what I've told you, but he responded little — perhaps to make me realize that I might have been blowing it up too much, perhaps not understanding how I felt. (Which I didn't either.) But he said it sounded like his night with me and Jeffrey and the girls before we went to Cannes, feeling incapable of doing anything about a situation deemed intolerable. Yes, Chuck, and more.

Tonight at dinner in Studio D we laughed and sang songs. We had been taken out to drinks after work by one of the young execs in the office and were happy. Work was over. The songs subsided and we sat in silence. Then Chuck said quietly:

"There were people crying at this table this morning. It's strange . . ."

"Yes. I was afraid that might have happened. Why did it?"

"Because of what you said to Jean. It was so —"

"Sarcastic?"

"Yes, sarcastic."

"Well that, I'm afraid, is the way I speak. It was meant to be absolutely sincere. Charmed was what I was, no more no less, and I could say only that. That she was hurt —"

"She was, and I didn't know what you were feeling. It's OK for me because you and I can hassle it out, but never for her."

"Chuck, believe it or not, take it or leave it, one of the reasons — and it was minor — was that I thought you might have wanted to be alone."

"Yes, but you were upset."

"Yes."

"She said she was sorry she hurt you, that she was sensitive too."

"I know, and I'm sorry she understood it that way."

"Well, I hope you'll talk about it sometime and not just file it away."

"Yes. I'll try." (A long pause.) "Well, I suppose I'll go and tell all my secrets to my typewriter. It's the only way I can do it now."

Chuck rose from the table and started toward the kitchen. Then he stopped, looked at me, and said, "I'm scared."

August 15, 1969

YESTERDAY was our last day of work. What was good, and different from leaving St. John's or Exeter, was that this being the last day, there was nothing special, either present or expressed or created, because we were leaving. Only toward the end of the day, which was filled with the usual work, did people in the office say good-bye. Our lady boss took us out for a *petit pot*, which is to say a *verre*, which is to say a drink at a café, and we talked and she was her unique self, always kidding you and laughing but always kind and sympathetic. She was sad to see us go. People in the office shaking hands rather shyly and not knowing what to say; others being practical and optimistic ("I will see you again someday, no?"), giving addresses — I have about ten now to write to in a while — and saying *á bientôt;* and others being sad and saying *grosse bise,* "big kiss." The two-cheeked version was carried out with finesse on some of the girls. On our lady boss it was a bigger one because in the great French way she offered three cheeks, one to have met you, two to leave, and the third either good luck or to grow on or *á bientôt.* I don't know, but I think it meant great affection and I was only surprised for a second. The men in the office said "Good-bye" and "If you ever need anything at all from France, write me or let me know and I will do it." Then the man in the mail section, old (who had seen Lindbergh), said,

"No good-byes. But when I have seen you for the last time, you will always be in my heart. I am too old to go to America, so that will have to do."

Like the eve of graduation, it was raining as we left the office, the end, and we ran home drenched, and not minding and thinking a lot of the eve of graduation — sitting in the dark under a dripping tree in my good clothes, soaking wet, staring at the bleachers and crying before I went back to the dance and cried and went home and cried. Now five days of gray skies while it is officially ending, the long end when I try to soak in Paris and realize that for the first time this summer I *know* Paris: museums and art galleries and a lot more awareness of what is happening. Like Exeter, you know it will soon be over when you have suddenly something to do each day before you leave; when you can practically see with your eyes every last day that you will spend in this place, the faces you have not known, the knowns you have not faced. Again.

Returning to Studio D, we found Herbert and Sheila had cleaned the apartment top to bottom for the first time since Jeffrey left. They had put a delicious tuna stew on the table, the first change from ham and cheese since our last grateful guests, the ones in between not having been so grateful or helpful. Herbert and Sheila and I went to see Z but it was too late so we wandered around. Sheila taught me the manual alphabet which has become my latest nervous habit. I have done it to myself all day, spelling with my hands everything I think of and see in Métro ads.

A final, wild word to try to tone down your impression of Herbert (which, I repeat, was mine before this summer). He and Sheila just returned from Morocco, and you know

what is there, and they brought back absolutely nothing of
that sort. Only those leather stools and some leather wine
sacks.

So we retired and this morning woke up to a big French
toast breakfast (ah, to have a woman in the house). Herbert
and Sheila and I went off to the Rodin museum which was
closed, then the modern art museum which was closed, and
then here for lunch and then again to Z. The walks — no
Métros, I felt like seeing Paris above the ground for once —
were beautiful, sort of overcast and gray but refreshing,
perfect temperature, the kind of Paris day you picture, if you
do. Along the river we talked: Herbert with his usual un-
interested look and comments, but you know he really is
interested and not blasé; bright Sheila with real interest and
enthusiasm.

Dinner on the Boulevard Saint-Germain — good steak,
wine, coffee — and then I ran alone down Paris streets, in
my *espadrilles* bought in the south of France and my American Levi's and my blue shirt which hasn't been washed in
two months . . . the beginning of a movie, with me the hero,
with music and this young stud running in bliss down a street
in Paris, and finally, as my wind catches up with me, I slow
to a walk down dark, quiet streets, the people are behind, and
the first title comes on: CHARLES TRUEHEART.

August 17, 1969

AFTER CHURCH today I sat down in the habitual American
Sunday drugstore and had my habitual *croque-monsieur* and
un demi and suddenly from behind came: "Will you buy me

a cup of coffee?" I turned around and it was Alter Kidd, the guy I had met four Sundays before. I shook his hand and spent two hours with him there, walking to the Etoile, then walking all the way over to the Rodin museum, where I met Herbert and Sheila. I can't tell you anything about Alter, except that he is the friendliest person I have known for a long time. I say that a lot. I say "the most" and "the best" and a lot of superlatives every day, but that is just the way each day is, always a superlative. You don't mean to insult any past experience or friendship, yet everything becomes a new superlative, a new phrase I have lived with today, for the means of grace and for the hope of glory.

But Alter was a glorious hopeful means of grace, and we did not talk profoundly or incisively (another old word) but just interestedly, for two hours. We helped each other, and then at the end, standing the two of us beneath trees in a park near Napoleon's tomb, near the Rodin museum, I said, knowing it would be no, why don't you come over for dinner tomorrow night, and he said no — just smiled and said he couldn't. He wouldn't even let me give him my address, he might have been tempted he said. I knew he was my friend, but a friend for the alone time, not associated with the rest of my life, just with sunny Sundays in Paris during the summer of 1969, when he was lonely and I was lonely, probably both of us lonely because we wanted to be. Not wanting it that way but it had to be so.

Rodin museum: quiet, gardens, buying prints and watching fish in a pond which held in the middle a statue of a man surrounded by four women and a baby. He was crouched on his hands and knees, looking down at tiny maidens, who lay twisted and writhing beneath him, all naked reflected in the pool. I sat with Herbert and Sheila and then we returned home and soon everyone slept, all of us in little corners on a hot Sunday afternoon, long and heavy.

When I awoke it was announced that we were going out to dinner. The sleep had been good but filled with nightmares, hate, fear, violence, alienation, me against everyone in the room. Afterward, standing in the courtyard with Chuck:

"I had a nightmare."

"What about?"

"Everyone in that room hated me."

"Including me?"

"Yes."

"Jesus, that's frightening."

"Yes. My head is really getting fucked up."

"I'm beginning to believe dreams . . . I guess you are too."

"I know."

The dinner was excellent, *escargots*, curry, coffee, conversation, talking and teaching the manual alphabet to Chuck and Al. Afterward, outside in the most fashionable section of Paris, the rue de Rivoli, fur-lined couples walked along the streets. Al and Chuck ripped open their shirts and revealed their new undershirts, pale blue type with narrow shoulder straps, the kind you always see in cartoons of beer-drinking Italians. Everyone took off clothes in front of stores, and ran toward the Tuileries gardens, Chuck and I there, then Sheila. Down the arcade, trucking, pants pulled up to his armpits, comes Herbert. Tourists stared as he trucked slowly across the streets to the rest of us standing in front of the gardens.

We laughed. They went to the gardens, inside, and I came back to write.

August 19, 1969

IT IS AFTERNOON of our last day here. Two months ago today we were leaving Washington, Chuck and I, on our way over, where things seemed different and foreign and frightening but always exciting. And now, as of about a week ago, we feel at home.

Chuck and I walked to the Jardin du Luxembourg yesterday and talked about old times. As we walked home we mimed out what we would do when we got home: driving along and turning on the car radio, pulling up to a McDonald's to have a hamburger, fries, and a thick shake.

So this is the last from the Studio D cubbyhole. It has been real.

I have an urge to turn this page into a *résumé* of the summer, where I could write to everyone who has spent the summer with me, with you and me, little flashes and phrases and memorable events in a stream of consciousness. But just as they were, they would be the little things, the important little things, and you never remember any of those, just the things you want to. If they are ever important, it is a coincidence; that they are real always is never easy to see, and no coincidence.

This also approaches another end and another beginning. The end is that I will stop writing every day soon, perhaps as I leave for school. It is something I will have to force myself to do, because I need to do it, not to break away from you but to break away from the habit of writing. It is more than a crutch sometimes, and it is often a discipline that is rigorous and self-imposed. Whatever it is, I have done it for what seems like a lifetime, and I would like to continue forever, but it is the old conflict of would and should, and I mustn't.

Home

Four

August 23, 1969

I WILL BE there, smiling, with you both as you read this. I could have told you, but my mind is bursting so I must write. Your baby sitter sounded gorgeous and delicious on the phone tonight.

"Sarah?"

"No, Sarah's not here."

"Well . . . who is this?" (My mother told me never to say that.)

"This is Linda Schjiuknmithyue."

"Oh, well, would you give a message to Mr. Gleason?"

I will probably find out that she is twenty-five or twelve. There is always Sarah.

Charles T. and I ate dinner with the Mannings on the last night in Paris. It was, as I expected, good to be there, Chuck a little flabbergasted — until he started drinking — with the surroundings, which are, I must admit, pretty impressive. It was sad to see the Mannings in the critical light. I am older and more cynical and perceptive without wanting to be. I

wanted to love them and overlook their manner and character, which I have always been able to do. They have
always been so interested in me and inquisitive but now it
was less so, perhaps because now I realized that *me* was the
most interesting topic of conversation, and they didn't. But
they were still gracious and generous, even though from a
long way back they had faults which I noticed only now.
Which I expect I will cease to notice as I get older. This ripe
stage is often maddening.

The plan to stay up all night and wander around Paris was
immediately canned because of the consumption of alcohol
and the general exhaustion of the last few days. We slept,
awoke in Paris, France, got on a jet plane, and in eight hours
were in New York City, a sleepless flight. New York, customs. As the man in the uniform, brusque, asked me to open
my bags, my fingers trembled and sweat poured off my face
though I had no reason to worry; he rummaged around and
finally said OK.

I looked up and caged behind a piece of plate glass, fresh
and excited, Mama and Papa waving frantically, and I waved
back in my customary aloof manner and went about the business of repacking. Chuck stood by and I had so much, what
with the damned typewriter, I said I'll take some of it up and
will you watch my shit, and he said yes. Out the door and
Father said, "Hi," grabbed the bags, and said, "We have five
seconds to catch the plane." What a more perfect welcome:
he had left me in June hurried and mad, now he greeted me
two months later hurried and nervous and flustered. I said,
"I have more stuff," and he said, "Go get it; hurry."

To Chuck, shaking his hand: "I have to run, I'm sorry, but
my father —"; up to Al: "Good-bye, I'll call, it's been great."

(Had it? Or do you just say it so that everyone's at ease. I mean I could have said, Well Al old boy, I still don't know a thing about you — sometimes it's been good and sometimes unbearable. But you just don't say that to anyone.) And I ran. Into a cab, rushing, plane missed, into another cab to LaGuardia to catch the shuttle. Finally I said, "Hi, Daddy," and he said, "Hi," but he was still flustered. That's my daddy and that's OK because he digs it. Could the Ambassador to Nigeria be serene? Would I even like him if he were?

It was good, home, got the dog at the kennel. Josh is visiting Grandmother in Richmond, so we could talk. Dinner, cheese that I brought them, and then we discussed going to Maine to see you. I countered many hassles and then an in-depth conversation about my relationship to them and you. Finally, after a bath in a bathtub, I crawled into a bed with clean sheets.

A pleasure to be home with the paternal and maternal hearts, fonder in his absence, steeled to the reality of his presence again. Life can continue with all its shit and all its flowers sprouting from the shit, again, again, again.

Father's day today: shopping and being with him, not a duty but a choice, a filial action neither exciting nor unbearable, but real and important, both of us in *espadrilles* at clothes stores. I bought a new blazer and my first gray suit and my first dress coat. Lunch at Clyde's, he in his striped T-shirt. Someone might have laughed because it was so funny to see him but he didn't notice. He was damned comfortable and proud and wise and he didn't give a shit and neither did I and we walked tall down M Street.

It all needs filling in, all of it, and there are more feelings that have zipped in and out. A few minutes ago I was alone

in the house, sitting on the porch — back in November you
were both there in your Sunday suits, yours was gray, wasn't
it, plaid with the old collar — when I lay back on the couch
and, "The Look of Love" came on the radio. The craving
started again, familiar and frustrating. I can only come up
with memories and fantasies.

Puck said the night before, "Your book won't sell unless
you get laid," and we laughed.

Mother came in, carrying an ashtray with a candle in it.
Sitting on top of the candle was a wilted flower. She said it
was her altar all summer, sitting on the windowsill above the
sink in the kitchen where she could watch it as she did the
dishes. The carnation that Charlie wore his last Sunday at
St. John's.

August 29, 1969

ORDINARILY I would have labeled the last four days in the
too-much-to-write-about category that gets me out of describ-
ing long, full, time periods. My visit with you in Maine was
too special to be labeled as anything. As I wrote in your
guest book, I will remember it.

It was a time of learning, about families and wives and
husbands and children. Despite the feeling that I felt at
home, that I felt a part, I often got the impression that
Galleon's Lap was even too special for someone who did not
always live there, that it becomes a home for anyone who
visits, but it is really yours, and it is to be loved.

You were not different people from Exeter days, or from
letters, but you transferred your uniqueness to a unique
place, and you became you intensified. I saw you, Ted, being

demanding and finicky, and shouting at your children. I saw that you too are not perfect, and believe me, that was a revelation. I had always thought you were, and it is better that I know you are not, because that makes you all the more human and lovable and identifiable. When I came home, I saw the same thing here. I know it happens and it is necessary.

We talked, late at night, about important things, and I learned a lot, and you did too. Nothing was solved, many things weren't even answered; but even though I expected them to be, relying on your perfection, it is good that they were not. It is good because they really *were;* they were discussed and thrown back and forth and digressed from and returned to and understood more. I am not going to stop smoking marijuana. You are not going to stop worrying about it. Mrs. Charles Trueheart is not going to walk through the door but she is there hiding behind some door somewhere, and I think I really did know that but was just impatient. We will all have problems and they will make us whole.

I begin to feel with a cramp in my stomach or a horde of butterflies gnawing like never before that everything is beginning again. I reach for Peter and Webster and Benjamin every day. I even start to telephone, but what would I say except that I miss you, I love you. (Would I say that?) I can't see you now, maybe later so we can talk about old times. Don't let the meat loaf. See you at the Exeter-Andover game. People I have cried with and laughed with all reduced to a telephone call or a beer while passing through town. This is not new, I have known it was coming for a long time, but now it begins to hurt like it was hurting last May, after a rapid-fire summer back to the real business.

There is no more to say now that I can express. Galleon's Lap was a great moment in my life, you know that.

August 31, 1969

THE BICKERING continues, and I am not immune. I must resort to escape. This household is worse than I thought, and today I am less optimistic about what's behind it than when I wrote you on Friday. Only because yesterday Mama apologized for having been mean the day before and then three hours later she was worse than ever. Today we couldn't even go to church together, everyone bitter and martyring themselves, Father and I going to church and Mother taking Josh to the Smithsonian.

Yesterday, as part of the escape, I drove to Baltimore to see the old school. Empty, deserted, and I saw myself trotting around here in a week's time. I couldn't even get into my dorm.

Maintenance man: "A rule is a rule . . . we gotta keep these locked up. You go talk to Mrs. Grumpleton."

"But just for a few minutes, couldn't I?"

"Look, I do my job and she does hers and we gotta keep it that way or we'll have a mess."

I can see how the American working mentality operates: no rocking the boat, no changes because it would disturb order. And Tricky Dick is in the Presidency. But I am no politico.

This morning I was wakened by Josh hitting me and tickling me which is not pleasant first thing. I remember being awakened at Galleon's Lap with a glass of fresh orange juice in the hand of a beautiful, blonde little girl. I hit Josh and that started the day.

PJL preached at church. I remember you heard he was "the hottest shit to come out of Virginia Seminary in ten years." It was a good sermon which I listened to attentively and so did everyone else. His command of the language is excellent; it is subtle, simple words which ring. The people at the church remembered me, the old war hero back for a visit, smiles, nods. Mrs. Lee waved until she caught my attention. I got a smile from PJL himself from the altar, which pleased me and embarrassed me since I thought ministers were never supposed to do that, show that they knew someone in the crowd.

I feel like coming back to school for another six or seven years. At least I know people and can profit a little more from having gone through all the shit to get to the good part. But that too is life — CT, the king of platitudes — and in the jungle of existence we must never lose our machetes.

September 2, 1969

WOULDN'T IT BE dramatic if I could say that this was the last one, the *end?* But it isn't and it won't be.

I'm leaving tomorrow, the car is loaded, my things are packed. Jennifer is unreached. My CLERGYMAN — EMERGENCY card is in the glove compartment, a gift from Willy Hills. Friends have been said good-bye to, families have asked me to stay with them. That is one of those things people say to you so many times, like "Where are you going

to college?" and "How was your summer?" Well-meant
questions but often repeated and hard to answer in an interesting way.

This morning in what should have been a dramatic moment of my life — but since things don't work that way it
wasn't — I registered for the draft. No drill sergeant, not one
military-industrial symbol, not even a complex one, just a nice
lady who told me what I had to know and explained about
CO and II-S. I filled out forms and she told me what to do
and I left. It was over just like that. Now I guess I'm a man,
but if there are many like me over there no wonder we have
problems.

Then I proceeded to H Street and paid a visit on Peter Lee.
God, I wish I could have gotten to know Colmore — always
looking at me as if he didn't trust me, his eyes going all over
my face and body in a sort of sizing-me-up way, always
smiling but in a sly way. He was there, back from his summer with a mustache and longer sideburns. Lee was happy
to see me and we chatted with a few intermittent silences,
both of us groping, about my summer. Things would be said
which would drop *plunk* on the floor and one of us would
have to start over again.

The rector is back Thursday. Lee happened to call him up
while I was there, and I could picture him talking because he
is a formidable, inimitable, affable man, and you don't forget
people with distinctive ways of being. That I think was what
took me so long to understand last April. He is distinct and
unique and viable, not a word you apply to a human being,
even though he is. His life-style is not only viable but real

and good and important and I'm glad we got past tie straight-
ening. To say the least.

The homeless waif is rapidly becoming so. It's almost
panic in my soul as I do things now for the last time. One of
my favorite pastimes is to go downstairs to the porch when
everyone is gone or asleep. I turn on the spotlights in the
yard and turn off the lights in the room, and it's like a screen
with no motion through the picture window. I put on Dylan
or Cohen and cry as I think of everything that is happening.
I am powerless to affect it.

I am the homeless waif suddenly on my own. I really don't
want it as much as I say I do. Things, little things, that
parents always did will now be up to me to do, and that's
hard, really hard. Now the breaking away has an intrinsic
excuse, there is really a departure. It is easier to rationalize,
for them and for me.

And tomorrow, like it or not, it all begins again. I have
thought about it for many days and have come to no conclusions except that I keep seeing and hoping it is Exeter 1969
again, where there was understanding and comfort and
friends. I know it won't be that way; there will be shit flung
in every direction for a long time until I become part of the
establishment. That's what it is, no matter how different.
When you're in the group, or into the place, you *are* the
establishment, and nobody bucks it.

Ernest Gillespie's graduation address comes to mind: "One
day you'll come back to Exeter, and we'll be glad to see you."

✿

September 5, 1969

TODAY I AM eighteen, and again, like when I was seventeen, I should be writing another poem. Perhaps I will this weekend when I go home, already from this place from this other window overlooking this other grass, perhaps because the time and events will be ripe for me to do so. It is my birthday today. This is the new beginning, for I will see Jennifer tonight. She is coming to dinner with my family and doesn't know the occasion. Tonight and tomorrow night will make or break whatever it is we have. What exactly we have, I don't know, but whatever it is, is now in a suspension of time and growth for both of us. Yes, what more can a *gentleman* say? He can say no more.

September 8, 1969

JESUS WALKED INTO a village at sunset. They knew him, in a strange way, though he was a stranger and they had never seen him before. He walked in alone and healed the sick and gave sight to the blind and then left. He was alone, and he had tried to help, and he had helped, and only one man was grateful, and that man watched Jesus walk off down the dusty road away from the valley. Jesus was alone.

I am not Jesus. At least, I am no more Jesus than any other, and yet there is nothing to Jesus but a man, any man, and the Jesus that is in him. John Harper preached a sermon Sunday, and I was there, home, and at church with the family. Joshua was an acolyte, and Mother and Father carried the elements and presented them to John Harper. Mother and Father and I ate the wafers — I chewed — and sipped the wine. Preachers have a way of giving you just enough to moisten your lips; it is jerked away just as it reaches your mouth. We sat down and prayed and I prayed for love between brother and mother and father and me and I prayed not to be alone very long.

The night before I sat alone — yes, by choice though I had no choice in my own mind — alone and very sad and very choked up because it is all so impossible. I was minding Joshua because my parents were dining with their closest friends. That was good because in public, especially in intimate public, they drink and they are funny and they forget all the hardships of the day.

Joshua was upstairs watching the budding Miss Americas. We decided they all had fat jelly thighs. I was lying on my back on the living room floor with my feet on the table. I was thinking. Joshua came down and started to be a little shit and I said, "Please don't bother me because I'm in a sad mood." He said, "What's the matter, did she slap you?" For once, I smiled, because it wasn't that simple. She didn't slap me, but I would have given my left arm for her to have done so. To Joshua, "No, it's just that everyone is nice to me, but no one loves me." It wasn't true except in my head. But I said it to him and he understood the distinction. He said, "But *I* love you," and I said, "Thank you."

We played go fish and watched TV and that was no permanent reconciliation, but it was affectionate and it happened. So we tickled each other on his bed and laughed at Miss Arizona singing opera and Miss Maine playing the clarinet and Bert Parks asking — the articulation test — one of the five finalists what she would tell her fourteen-year-old sister "now that she is entering the 'Now' generation." Bert:

"You do have a fourteen-year-old sister, isn't that right?" She:
"Yes." Then she stood up and said, "Well, I can't tell my
sister anything because she has brain damage, but for *other*
fourteen-year-olds . . ." and Parks just about swallowed his
microphone. I explained what had happened to Josh, but I'm
not sure if it sunk in.

Jennifer came over Friday night for birthday dinner and
was quiet and polite. I felt it was strained and then after
dinner, just as Papa announced that he was going upstairs
to study Nigeria, I said, "Wait, I want to read you a letter,
all of you. I want you to hear it together. It's from Teddy."
I read it out loud, slowly, because it was perfect and it said
the true things. When I was done, both parents reacted by
saying it was beautiful which I know they believed. They
were nervous because I had read it in front of Jennifer, so
they hastily picked up ashtrays and glasses and went to bed.
Jennifer, *comme toujours*, silent.

So when absolute silence had settled over our little evening
of fun and laughs, I said: "Do you think I should have read
it?" She: "Do you think you should have?"

I dropped it. I started talking about how she never
reacted to anything, and she said she just didn't know how
she was feeling. Teddy, I can't do her or us justice now, four
days later. We talked for hours about everything, but it
was mostly me talking. Talking about what part of you really
is you, and how my parents were different with her there
than they really are, and she listened and asked questions
while I told her my philosophy of life. I said I wanted to
hear her and she said the best way was to talk myself. "Tell

me in detail," she said, "your entire summer." So I did. Chris, the Evening, the Jean and Chuck Affair start to finish, with me being more honest with myself about the latter than I have ever been. Concluding nothing. She did not react at all, just listened, soaked it all in. I said, "My God, can't you do something?" And she said she was reacting but only inside. I conceded, though I wouldn't now, that if it was my bag to rap about everything going on inside, then it was hers to react inside and say nothing. She finally told me about some people she met this summer and a boy "who never reads, never uses his head, and just lives for crew and he's going to be a chemical engineer and that is that and he's a neat kid." I said that I wasn't afraid of being a narcissist or a masochist.

I told her, in intermittent comments, how I felt about her and how I wasn't sorry about anything I had ever said to her even though I always felt she was uncomfortable when I started being profound. She said no, she was never uncomfortable. We went to the kitchen and had Frescas and went through all the kitchen drawers looking at the instruments. When she left, I read a Peanuts book until 3 AM to bring myself down to another level, so to speak. That did no good because I was seeing the most incredibly truthful religious existential allusions in every cartoon.

September 14, 1969

I KNOW NOW. She will, she does, she has reacted, inside. And if that is her way of doing it, great. She didn't send a letter; she wrote to me. Why? Because it was inside. She told me about it and that was good enough. I wouldn't have expected any more. She did react, to me, to your letter to me, to everything, and she continues to. Sunday, leaving —

"When's a good time to call?"

"When are you calling, this week?"

"Yes. I'm getting a phone installed, and I want a chance to use the phone and my excuse will be to find out your address at Barnard."

"Oh, in the evenings."

"Like six or like nine?"

"Like six."

"Six it is."

"And I'll be able to get your phone number."

"Yes."

"And have a good drive back."

"And you to New York."

"Promise I'll hear from you before I leave?"

"Promise."

Backward, down the driveway and home. It was simple and there was nothing more. But it was suddenly no longer raspberry juice; now it was raspberry Jell-O. And Jennifer and I were a couple of raspberries.

September 17, 1969

A WHILE AGO, a premonition of death. I was not feeling sorry for myself, or particularly morose, but I was reading my history and suddenly three images came in quick succession:

Me lying in a muddy gully in Vietnam with dried blood and flies and my mother crying.

Mother and father and brother dying when their ship goes down in the Atlantic.

You and Anne crying deeply at someone's funeral.

I return for the final weekend with parents this weekend, and then I'm on my own. I am scared. No doubt about it. You don't wish for things like Mother coming in at six to find your dirty clothes and getting a fried egg cooked and not broken, until you don't have them. I see myself sleeping in the back seat of the Mustang on Christmas night with a frozen turkey TV dinner in my lap, heated with the car cigarette lighter.

September 22, 1969

FRIDAY: A letter received from Chuck. Excerpts from a letter which was meant more deeply than mine to him. Chuck doesn't write often or much, but he writes when he has something to say, and there is no bullshit involved.

> Maybe that's the point of separation now — it's not really spatial or temporal (wow), but just that we're all trying to hack so much and it really is an alone time . . .
>
> And then there is a thing which is at the center of me now, a thing which I can't quite fit (why?) into all the things I have to say to you. This is Alice. I took a bus from Cambridge up to see her the weekend of the 5th and she and I spent three days of total exposure to each other, and to her whole group of friends there. I still can't and won't get far outside those days and describe. It's just so much easier and at this point more accurate to see it through a romantic lens now. Because it was a very romantic thing — much the fulfillment of what

we said to each other in scattered letters over the summer. I
can say only that there was much sun and rain and skin to taste
and huge eyes and ups and downs, all in three very intense
days.

Please accept all this — and for now and Christ knows maybe
forever that's what it's all about. I have a warm feeling that
everything I say to you, you already know. I could sit here
and sputter all the truths and beauties that Jeffrey spoke of and
that you and I have seen together, but like I said I know that
you know and for all this I am grateful to whoever and whatever we are grateful to. Christ, and so much more, Charlie.
And peace to you too. You know.   CHUCK

Saturday: Mostly work of one kind or another, in preparation for our party Sunday night, and in preparation for a
party given for us by the Bradleys Saturday night. The
Bradleys are close family friends with the daughter baby
sitter named Camille. Discussions with Dad about car
insurance, snow tires, antifreeze, and other matters of mutual
boredom.

At six-thirty I went to the Bradleys' and underwent the
expected rigmarole. All the guests (40) were old members
of the S Street house during the forties, which housed a
group of select bachelors and which was actually not on S
Street but at various places around the capital, and was at
N Street when my father was there. There were others, old
friends from the pre-Charlie era when life was free and fun.
I heard all versions of the story of Mr. Howe's deep voice
scaring me to death every time he came over — plus other
stories. People I hadn't seen in many years, people who had
heard about me through God knows what channels. The
conversations were usually of this nature; as a matter of fact,
almost without exception, they were of this nature:

Silence. Uh, are you Charlie? Oh, yes. (Smug grin.) My
God, the last time I saw you, you were this tall. (Indicates
height of a grasshopper's knee.) Oh . . . say, uh, are you in
college now? Oh, yes . . . I'm at Johns Hopkins. Oh, really,
close by, eh, yuk yuk. Yes. Silence. Uh . . . medical school?
No, no . . . uh, international relations. Oh, yuk yuk, following
in your father's footsteps, eh? Huh huh, yes. And, uh, when
are you going out to Nigeria, Christmas? No, no, not till
next summer probably. Oh, I see, well . . . where are you
going to be during vacations? Oh, huh huh, bumming up
and down the east coast, visiting friends. Oh, well listen, you
know in our house we always have a bed for you, I mean any
time. I appreciate that. I certainly will remember. No, no,
I mean it. I mean you can do whatever you want, huh huh,
no questions asked. Oh, yuk yuk, good. Thank you. Well,
I think I'll go find the bar, heh heh.

Accordingly, Camille and I grasped the first opportunity
and went out and turned on under a tree in a nearby park.
And then returned. If it was ever for escape, it was Saturday
night. But I don't mean to belittle or degrade these people.
They are all, almost all, wonderful friendly people. I couldn't
be more grateful for their hospitality. And I will, with my
long list of names, drop in on a lot of them this year. I suppose I am just too intolerant of boring situations. And this
was one.

Sunday: Punted church because of business and I felt it
when eleven o'clock rolled around. I won't try to draw any
conclusions about that. More packing and rooting out junk
all day, and then our party at five.

About a hundred people came, almost all State Department
people, many of whom I hadn't seen since the time when I

was that tall. Same conversations, different people, and when it first started I suddenly couldn't stand it. I went with a screwdriver to the basement. I overcame my fears somehow (probably visions of a ruined career in the Foreign Service or something equally absurd) and went upstairs and rapped with a lot of people. The conversations became more lengthy and I became more drunk (still no immunity to gin and tonics) and listened to people tell me their views on the youth movement and how fucked it was. I have a weakness of agreeing with them because it is too hard to argue with someone over thirty. That is *true*, unless they are special people. I told one woman, when she said, "Charlie, are you smoking too? Larry's on the weed and it's terrible," that yes, he and I used to smoke on their roof in Saigon so it's not new. She dug that immensely.

It was not easy to leave. House empty and smell of drink and smoke, the hired waiters cleaning up and we three sitting saying good-bye. Just then, I began to feel the end as it is really felt. Nothing special was said, insurance policy numbers, explanations of the forty thousand mile checkup. I said it would not be easy to be alone. They understood, and I think they were sad too. It was a beginning for them. A lot of the past had disappeared.

Just before the party, my father telephoned old friends in London, very good close friends who had put me up in their flat this summer, good people of old days. I listened as my father talked to them, and I felt for him. Daddy started with "Edouardo!" The answer was "Hi, Bill." Very cool. The conversation was that way. Edouardo at the other end of the line was very restrained and said, "Fine" — no congratulations or mention of Lagos. As Father and I walked downstairs, I said, "That was very strange," and he said, "Yes, he seemed kind of cool, didn't you think?" I said, "Yes, it's too bad," and then we entered the fray. That was probably why I couldn't take it at first, why I cried for them over my screwdriver in the basement.

Sunday afternoon, I buried two of our three gerbils in the backyard. I did it alone, and I made up my own impromptu service on the hill at 5149. Death, and it even rained.

Tomorrow morning I'm going back to Washington for the swearing-in Wednesday. They leave Wednesday night and I come back here that afternoon. I don't want to be there when it happens. Edward flies by box tomorrow. He is an old dog now, and I hope he makes it. He's been watching me all these years and he knows more than any of us what it's like.

September 25, 1969

IT WAS EARLY 1958. Daddy was in London, and Mother and I were staying in Paris, at a kind of hotel-apartment, because we had already moved out of our house. We had our orders to go to Turkey, and that's why we had moved out. Mother decided to go to London to meet Daddy. I said I wanted to go, and she said no, that I couldn't. So I was to stay with Marc, my French school friend, at his country house. She took me out there and stayed for a drink and left. I knew she had gone, but it didn't dawn on me until late that afternoon that she was really no longer there, and that she was probably already on the plane to London. And here I was, American, alone with a French family who were nice to me but basically strangers. She was a pretty housewife and he was a portly shoe manufacturer. Marc was my age, a little dark-haired school chum. As soon as I realized that she had gone, I became hysterical, screaming and crying and making an absolute asshole of myself in front of Mr. and Mrs. and Marc. It took from about four in the afternoon until seven or eight, dinnertime, to calm me down. That was finally achieved by getting Marc and me dressed up in costumes, Marc as a French peasant boy, and me as an Arabian sultan with baggy silk pants and a puffed out shirt. I whimpered as they dressed me up and kept asking when she would be back and that she had left me without knowing and that she wouldn't come back. I thought about my outburst most of the weekend, and sure enough, Sunday night Mother and Daddy came to pick me up.

The James Madison Room of the State Department with all the old friends and the African officials and Daddy's weeping secretary and Grandmother and me and Joshua and Mother. Lots of cameras and microphones. Elliot Richardson made a speech about Nigeria and Daddy which was superb and eloquent. Then Daddy, after taking the oath, spoke briefly. He and Richardson shook hands and smiled for the cameras. Mother and Daddy kissed and Daddy said in his speech that he couldn't have made it without the help of two women, his mother and his wife, and I smiled. The night before, from my bed reading, I heard "God damn it, Phoebe . . ." The subject of their argument is old and meaningless. It could have been any subject at all and I would have heard the same. We drank coffee and pictures were taken and they brought the movie cameras two inches from our faces. I can't imagine what they did with them.

But I beamed and looked cool. I was proud because ever since I became aware of bureaucracies and ambassadors and promotions and honors and formal things, which was earlier than most people (to my ultimate demise since I did a hell of a lot of bragging in Saigon), ever since, I have waited for the day when this would happen. I always wanted it to be big and important and it was. I saw Jonathan Moore and we shook hands and smiled. "This is the day," I told him, "and I want to thank you." He said, "Nonsense, this should have happened a long time ago." The Truehearts formed a receiving line, shaking hands with everyone, and everyone said to me that I would like Nigeria, and here again I mean every last one, which proves my thesis that adults are basically boring, unimaginative people.

(I just lit a cigarette with a match from Galleons Lap. By the way, shouldn't that be possessive, Galleon's Lap? I mean, I don't want to be picayune, but after all, if your sloppy guests leave their damn shoes all over the living room, you might as well make an effort to spell things correctly.)

We came down from the James Madison Room and climbed into our borrowed brown rattling station wagon and drove home, mile a minute, Grandmother's mouth about two miles a minute. "I remember when Charlie was . . ." Mustang low on gas, sitting on Tilden Street, the Peugeot, or "Poojoe" as you say, shipped that morning, and arrived home. I was sent on errands for an hour or so, then we came home, or I came home with the Ambassador. We ate on the lawn (sandwiches because there was no furniture or food or silver or china). Then there was total chaos all afternoon while I tried to get away and Mama and Papa said no. Packing and deciding and chucking out and picking up things and answering the telephone. Alice drove by by chance and saw me and said Hello, looking wide-eyed and pretty as ever. I finally got in the car and drove away. There were no tears, standing on the front lawn, just be good and Mother: "Please try and come out after Christmas." Then I drove off, waving as men in dirty overalls stood around with a million questions. Edward is in a box flying over Africa, and Josh, I guess, was in the backyard playing baseball.